A Balanced Approach
To Employment Counseling

The Medicine Wheel

✦

A Balanced Approach To Employment Counseling

Lily Nowak

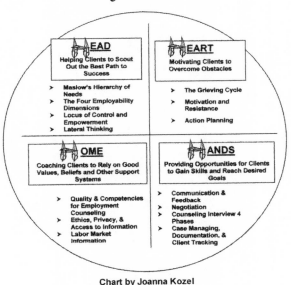

Chart by Joanna Kozel

Developed by Lily Nowak in conjunction with Oteenow
Employment & Training Society

iUniverse, Inc.
New York Lincoln Shanghai

The Medicine Wheel
A Balanced Approach To Employment Counseling

iUniverse books may be ordered through booksellers or by contacting:

iUniverse
2021 Pine Lake Road, Suite 100
Lincoln, NE 68512
www.iuniverse.com
1-800-Authors (1-800-288-4677)

The views expressed in this work are solely those of the author and do not necessarily reflect the views of the publisher, and the publisher hereby disclaims any responsibility for them.

ISBN: 978-0-595-44396-3 (pbk)
ISBN: 978-0-595-88725-5 (ebk)

Printed in the United States of America

Dedication

This work is for those people blessed with helping spirits who focus their strengths to guide others to better places.

I am proud to have had such support from the Oteenow staff who helped me to understand what a wonderful tool the Medicine Wheel really is.

The following people deserve credit for their work on this guide:

-Donna Potts-Johnson, Jim Badger, Gilman Cardinal, Myron Sparkling-eyes—members of the Oteenow Board of Directors who shared their insight into First Nations culture and traditions thereby deepening my respect for their esteem for all things spiritual and all things natural.

-Clayton Kootenay, Executive Director of Oteenow Employment and Training Society gave his support to this effort and made it happen. Thank you Clayton!

-Jackie Loyer, a Cree Elder with lots of counseling experience, whose knowledge of the Medicine Wheel and suggestions for cultural clarity provided a solid base from which the '4 H' model could fly. She also provided the head, heart, hands and home graphics for the medicine wheel.

-Paulette Neigel whose proof reading and editing skills give this book a professional tone. She not only has a way with words but is also a talented artist!

-Julie Milne whose experience and expertise in the field of human resources were invaluable.

-Joanna Kozel for her early formatting work and clever creation of a chart showing how the chapters of the book fit into the quadrants of the medicine wheel.

Like the stone Medicine Wheels etched into the old Indian hunting grounds, may this approach to helping those in need serve to guide the helpers in their missions.

Acknowledgements and Evolution of this Work

This guide is the culmination of approximately twenty years of experience working with Human Resources Departments called Worker Services (counseling) and Labor Market Adjustment (employer services) as well as consulting with various Aboriginal organizations.

In addition to the ageless knowledge known as the Medicine Wheel, the basis for this work was already developed by experts in counseling, business practices and negotiating. This was gleaned from training packages developed by Human Resources Development Canada (as it was known in those days) to train the trainers from all the provinces in Canada.

Many 'training for trainers' lectures were provided by guest professors to the Alberta region including Norm Amundsen and Bill Borgen from University of British Columbia, Dave Redikopp of Concordia College in Edmonton and William Schultz for his proposed code of ethics for employment counselors, among others. Publications that were used as references for the training packages included Tom Peters' approach to business management, especially his famous 'change exercise' chock full of human behavioral analysis as well as Roger Fisher's, William Ury's and Bruce Patton's book on negotiation: <u>Getting To Yes</u>. There were others as mentioned in the various chapters of this work and in the bibliography.

Credit must go to Darlene MacDonald, Manager of Worker Services who strived to establish top-notch training teams to train employment counselors in Alberta and to the late Jeff Keto along with Judy Berg, Managers of Labor Market

Adjustment who developed employer services training teams that were second to none in Canada (including Nova Scotia).

These government departments are now defunct but the superior work from counseling and employer services training is captured in this guide as a vital part of the Medicine Wheel approach to employment counseling. The four quadrants of the Medicine Wheel provide a structure for "balance" in identifying and resolving employment needs and barriers.

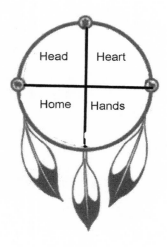

Table of Contents

Introduction

The goal of this handbook is to present a simple systematic approach to employment counseling using the Aboriginal Medicine Wheel as the lens through which a client's employment needs will be explored and suitable solutions found to help the client achieve balance in employment related areas.

Employment counseling is essentially the creation of a trusting relationship between a counselor and the client. This trust allows a client to identify his or her own employment needs or advise why he or she is unable to seek or find work. **These problems usually relate to the need for balance in some or all of the four quadrants in the Medicine Wheel. Employment counseling also provides an opportunity for an employment counselor to share employment information, advise clients about community resources and refer clients to partners who possess appropriate expertise and/or programs that will help the client accomplish his or her employment plans.**

The Medicine Wheel, long known by Aboriginal communities for promoting balanced lifestyles, brings cultural clarity to employment issues as well as other challenges facing Aboriginal counselors and clients. When the Medicine Wheel is combined with the analytical approach established by the four employability dimensions, the best possible path through the realm of client needs becomes clear. These tools will be critical for the Aboriginal employment counselor.

To foster understanding of the concepts in the Medicine Wheel, basic terminology has been adopted to label each of the four quadrants: **Head** (intellectual), **Heart** (emotional), **Hands** (physical), **Home** (spiritual).

This "**4-H**" approach was advocated by Human Resources Development Canada over a decade ago in training their employment counselors. It has since been used successfully in employment counseling and fits perfectly with the Medicine Wheel concept used in Aboriginal communities.

It has long been recognized that Aboriginal Elders have a wealth of wisdom they can share even though some are not necessarily educated by European standards. This wisdom will continue to be called upon by many people experiencing complications in their lives. 'Employment counseling' deals with supply and demand issues in the local labor market, with an appreciation of how labor market conditions impact on unemployed clients seeking work. A counselor's understanding of how labor markets function would likely be improved if she or he is a graduate from high school. Most people seeking work soon learn what their chances are of finding it after much trial and error.

The Medicine Wheel model for counseling these clients helps job seekers to take a more direct path to meaningful employment. Since Aboriginal employment counselors also become *role models* for their clients, they should have a good understanding of the Aboriginal culture through the teachings of the Medicine Wheel and may approach local Elders to help them learn more, if necessary. This handbook shows how the Medicine Wheel serves like a 'scout' blazing a trail through the maze of client's barriers and needs to desirable employment. Employment counseling is only a sliver of the vast array of issues that could be explored using the Medicine Wheel as a guide.

Generally, employment counselors aim to help clients to

- identify their own employment needs;
- choose appropriate solutions through mutual agreement between clients and employment counselors;
- plan appropriate action steps to reach solution; and
- implement appropriate action steps to reach solution.

In accomplishing these aims, employment counselors must understand their responsibility is limited to

- facilitating interviews to help clients to identify their own employment needs and/or barriers;
- presenting an appropriate array of options to clients for solving their employment needs and/or suggesting who has the expertise to overcome employment barriers, if necessary;
- helping clients make an action plan to address employment needs or making referrals as needed; and

- coaching and mentoring clients while they implement action plans and help to make adjustments as required to ensure appropriate solutions are achieved.

Challenges facing counselors and clients may be internal or external. In the final analysis, each challenge will be examined with the help of the Medicine Wheel.

This handbook will be written in accordance with a chapter outline to provide consistency and clarity. The chapter outline will contain the following headings:

- **Chapter Goal**—To achieve balance in …
- **Background**—Important issues about the chapter topic are covered.
- **Motivation**—Why do you need to understand this?
- **Presentation**—How does it work?
- **Examples**—Show me!
- **Summary and Key Points**—What is most important about this issue?
- **Self-Test Questions**—How well do I understand this?

1

A Traditional Aboriginal Approach to a Balanced Lifestyle—The Medicine Wheel

Chapter Goal—To achieve balanced behavior.

Background—Important issues about this topic follow.
Important issues include the four distinct points of view provided by the Medicine Wheel for the purpose of examining needs in each of the four employability dimensions.

The Medicine Wheel provides a way to look at human behavior and interactions among people. It conforms with the Aboriginal belief that all natural things in the world come in 'fours'. For the purposes of employment counseling, the quadrants of the Medicine Wheel cover intelligence or 'head', emotions or 'heart', physical being or 'hands', and spiritual being or 'home'. These Medicine Wheel quadrants also provide four distinct points of view to examine employment issues in each of the four Employability Dimensions. The goal of such examination is to achieve balance through the satisfaction of clients' employment needs.

Motivation—Why do you need to understand this?

The Medicine Wheel employment counseling model in conjunction with the Four Employability Dimensions provides a reliable approach to help clients identify and resolve their employment needs with the help of an employment counselor. It also helps employment counselors to present the best options for clients to overcome employment barriers. For the purpose of this guide, there is a clear distinction between 'employment' and 'career' counseling which is addressed in chapter two. It is enough for now to clearly understand that 'employment' counselors do not need to have a university degree as do 'career' counselors because employment counselors refer their clients to experts as the need to do so arises.

The "4-H" counseling approach is a client-centered approach that means:

1. Early intervention is needed to address clients' employment needs.

2. Clients recognize their needs with the help of counselors.

3. Clients choose the best ways of addressing their needs with the help of counselors.

4. Clients participate in the entire counseling process and make their own decisions based on what they think is best for them with the help of counselors.

5. Counselors discharge their duty to clients by ensuring they present a variety of options to clients from which they can choose, having regard to the client's personal and community resources.

Presentation - How does it Work?

The Medicine Wheel & the "4-H" Counseling Approach

Education & Training

Knowledge produces behaviours
that are expressed differently
by individuals with different
personality traits.

Attitudes

Emotions produce behaviours
that are expressed differently
by individuals with different
personality traits.

Medicine Wheel
Intellectual
4 H: Head

Medicine Wheel
Emotional
4 H: Heart

Medicine Wheel
Spiritual
4 H: Home

Medicine Wheel
Physical
4 H: Hands

Values & Beliefs

Spiritual values and beliefs originate
from "home" where the upbringing or
environment experienced by the
person forms the "context" influencing
personal behaviour (sometimes irrational)
that are expressed differently by individuals
with different personality traits.

Physical Skills, Innate Abilities

Skills and abilities (including talents) produce
behaviours that are expressed differently by
Individuals with different personality traits.

Examples—Show me!

1. I only have a grade six education (head/intellectual). My Mom and Dad needed money so I went to work as soon as I was fourteen years old (home/spiritual). Our whole family drank a lot (hands/physical).

2. I am good at making cabinets and carving wood. I would like a job doing that (hands/physical) but I only have a grade eight education (head/intellectual) and cannot get into apprenticeship.

3. I have three children and no one to look after them (barrier/home/spiritual because a trustworthy babysitter is needed and the client will need to take the initiative to find childcare while the counselor may help to finance the childcare arrangement).

4. I married a Jehovah Witness and I can no longer be an emergency medical technician because I cannot give anyone a blood transfusion (home/spiritual belief). I need to be retrained.

Summary and Key Points—What is most important about this issue?

Each quadrant of the Medicine Wheel provides a distinctive point of view of client needs. The "head" deals with intellectual issues including education and the client's ability to learn. Slow learners or smart clients need to be assisted by counselors to find appropriate schools and training institutions that will help them to develop as much as possible while at the same time choosing occupations that will provide sufficient challenge to them and lead to success.

Two basic emotions affect the heart and give rise to all other feelings: fear and love. Fear leads to hatred and cripples a spirit so that clients end up as failures. Love strengthens and heals the spirit leading clients to success. Employment counselors must be able to recognize if clients are unhappy, depressed or anxious and unable to control their fears. These clients should be referred to psychologists or other certified counselors for help. Employment counselors can only deal with clients who have needs related to employment and to help them to become job ready. "Hands" include all skills and talents learned or possessed by the client. This includes skills like the trades, or professional skills such as playing musical instruments, singing, surgery, chemistry, cooking and weather forecasting, to name a few.

Clients need to be encouraged to share information about their skills and talents, as these areas will usually point to careers that will be satisfying to them.

"Home" is where the client has formed all of his values, beliefs and experiences that affect his/her spiritual health. It also provided him/her with an environment, which either helped or hindered the client to develop spiritually.

Self-Test Questions—How well do I understand this?

1. A man who is 47 years old was laid off from his job as he is no longer physically able to work as a laborer. He admits to you that he cannot read and write because he never went to school at all. Describe how each quadrant of the Medicine Wheel is involved and discuss the possible solutions you might suggest for the client.

2. A woman in a wheel chair has a grade four education. Her husband was killed a month ago in a car accident and she needs to go to work to support her four children. She is still in shock over the accident but she has no one at all to help her since her Mother and Father are dead and she has no siblings. Her husband's family has 10 children with only one small income and a three-room house in which they all live. Describe how each quadrant of the Medicine Wheel is involved and discuss the possible solutions you might suggest for the client.

3. An eighteen-year-old girl is living in the streets and on drugs. She comes to you begging for help to get off the streets and find a good job. She needs to do this because child welfare has taken her baby away from her and put the infant into a foster home until she gets her act together. They are willing to participate in paying for some of the interventions she will need but she must come to them with a detailed action plan that is approved by the employment counselor she will be working with. Describe how each quadrant of the Medicine Wheel is involved and discuss the possible solutions you might suggest for the client.

2

Legal Limitations in Employment Counseling

Chapter Goal—To achieve balance in the proper delivery of employment counseling to clients including that:

- *Employment counseling relies on clients to identify their own employment issues using the Medicine Wheel as a self-exploration guide.*

- *Employment counselors recommend the best options from which clients may choose to satisfy their employment needs or overcome employment barriers.*

Background—An Important issue about this topic follows.
An important issue on this topic is that employment counselors are expected to know the limits of their employment counseling roles and not exceed them. Partners certified in various areas of expertise such as education, medicine, religion and spirituality to name a few, would be summoned to assist the client when required.

The role of an employment counselor is to help clients identify their personal employment needs and to share current labor market information to help them properly address these employment needs. Employment "needs" refer to the need to make an appropriate career decision, the need for skills training and the need for learning how to do job search. At the same time it is also important for employment counselors to recognize barriers to employment that the client might have. Barriers are circumstances that prevent a client from accessing employment. Barriers may include a lack of education, emotional disturbances or illnesses, disabilities, addictions, or crippling systems of values and beliefs. External assistance is usually required and appropriate referrals would be made accordingly.

Career counselors are those persons possessing university degrees that enable them to provide more in-depth assistance to deal with clients' needs and barriers. Employment counselors do not require a university degree because they are only required to recognize that barriers exist and refer clients to appropriate specialists for help. Employment counselors are also required to be familiar with all the suitable options available for satisfying clients' needs and to present them to clients with recommendations. Clients are responsible for selecting those deemed best for themselves.

Motivation—Why do you need to understand this?

Employment counselors attempting to deliver interventions in areas where they are not certified to do so would be exceeding their capacity and authority as well as the mandate of the organization for which they work. This creates a situation where the employment counselor could be held legally responsible for malpractice.

Presentation—How does it work?

Employment counseling uses the four quadrants of the Medicine Wheel in conjunction with the four employability dimensions in a systematic approach to address a client's employment needs and, where barriers exist, refer them to specialty services if necessary.

What does an employment counselor do?

Employment counselors' roles have been determined by the client and organization's expectations. The roles will be grouped under four quadrants of the Medicine Wheel as follows:

HEAD

- presenting appropriate options to clients, helping them to explore them and choose one they think is best for them
- helping clients to analyze their own situation so they appreciate the consequences of their choices
- knowing funding sources that may be available and arranging funding
- keeping up to date on local labor market information

- knowing what community resources are available including all local partners and the services or programs they offer
- developing professionally and personally as well as participating in employment counseling-related conferences and meetings

HEART

- Mentoring and supporting clients as they implement their action plans
- Encouraging clients to actively participate in carrying out their action plans
- Empathizing with clients as they deal with both failure and success

HANDS

- Conducting themselves in a professional manner so as to present a good image of themselves and their organization
- Communicating clearly
- Helping clients to organize logical steps into action plans toward employment goals
- Adjusting the steps in an action plan as needed
- Documenting and tracking client progress
- Working with partners to form networks to support clients in dealing with employment related issues
- Sharing labor market information in a timely way

HOME

- Providing a safe environment for client meetings and counseling sessions
- Protecting clients' privacy and helping to gain access to necessary information
- Ensuring clients are aware of why information is collected and obtaining their written permission to share it with appropriate partners as required
- Helping clients to take the best advantage of cultural choices available to them

To be an effective employment counselor one must have good self-esteem and be able to build trusting relationships with clients.

Building Self Esteem & Trusting Relationships

1. **HEAD**

    - Be courageous—take risks and try new things that could lead to growth (remember the most effective learning is from making a mistake).

    - Believe that differences provide a chance to learn and grow. Try to see the world from the perspective of your client to better appreciate his/her situation.

    - Be open to suggestions for improvement but at the same time be assertive—not stubborn. Have good reasons for defending your position.

2. **HEART**

    - Authenticity—be honest and authentic about your feelings, thoughts and actions (as this leads to integrity).

    - Spontaneity—risk showing feelings that empathize with client.

    - Trust yourself—believe in yourself to the point where you can honestly express your feelings and emotions without regret.

    - Understanding—differences can lead to isolation because the differences are not understood or accepted by others. Children in schools who are isolated may be teased and bullied and this could lead to violent reactions from the victim. Clients suffering from this type of abuse may need to be referred to specialists to help them deal with these issues.

3. **HANDS**

    - Commitment—promise yourself to carry out certain actions and reach certain goals that you have set for yourself.

    - Congruency—"walk the talk" or "practice what you preach."

    - Listening—do not complain, judge, defend, or offer solutions until you have heard what a client has to say.

- Objectivity—when your feelings get in the way, you will not be able to recognize the main issues that need attention.

4. **HOME**

- Integrity—set your personal values because they are important to you and at the same time respect organizational values.

- Responsibility—own your own feelings, your actions, your values and be ready to defend them without forcing them on others; own your mistakes but use them as a lesson for the future. In this way, you turn a loss into a win for yourself.

- Keep your word—strive to keep any promises you have made.

Examples—Show me!

1. A client asks for and receives current, in-depth local labor market information from an employment counselor because this is his or her responsibility as an employee of the employment organization for which he or she works. No referrals to outside agencies are necessary.

2. A client who has only passed grade 8 in school but needs grade 10 to get into an apprenticeship course is referred to an educational institution to go to school. The employment counselor is not a teacher responsible for educating clients.

3. A client is referred to an agency that has addictions counselors to work with the client. This referral was made by the employment counselor even though the employment counselor is a trained addictions counselor also. The reason for the referral is that the employment counselor is not hired to be an addictions counselor and the organization for which he or she works has no responsibility to perform addictions counseling.

4. Clients may need financial assistance to arrange for child care, or transportation, etc.. In such cases, employment barriers may be overcome through the efforts of the clients themselves with the help of the employment counselor.

Summary and key points—What is most important about this issue?

Employment counseling deals with clients' employment needs. Employment counselors may assist them by sharing information, presenting options and providing financial assistance as they act to satisfy their needs. When employment counselors encounter barriers to employment, they must decide if clients can overcome these on their own (babysitting, transportation, etc.) with some assistance from the employment counselor, or if they need outside expertise to overcome barriers, (education, addictions, doctors, etc.) in which case, the employment counselor will make an appropriate referral and provide other support as required.

Self-Test Questions—How well do I understand this?

1. As far as an employment counselor is concerned, what is the difference between employment needs and barriers to employment?

2. What could an employment counselor do if she or he finds that a client is hard of hearing and has bad arthritis yet he wants to work as a truck driver?

3. What are the qualities of a good employment counselor?

4. Why is it so important for an employment counselor to "walk the talk?"

5. How can differences between the client and the counselor's perspective work to mutual advantage?

6. Why is it important for an employment counselor to know the limits of their counseling roles?

3

Maslow's Hierarchy of Needs

Chapter Goal—To achieve a relevant approach to challenges facing the client, thereby helping him/her to achieve balance as the client deals with more complex needs.

Background—Important issues about this topic follow.
Important issues for consideration in this chapter are that clients may have such consuming needs that they cannot deal with anything else until those needs are satisfied. Maslow has put these needs in order of importance to people. "Maslow's Hierarchy of Needs" says that if clients are homeless, without food or worried for their safety, they will not be able to deal with their employment needs until these more urgent needs to survive are resolved. Organizations must recognize these are client priorities and refer them to suitable partners (example: addictions counselors if they are suffering from addictions) before asking them to make career decisions or go into training. The following shows how people deal with their needs (in ascending order) starting at the bottom with the need for survival of the physical body.

The person's need for self-actualization

The person's need for self-esteem

The person's need for love

The person's need for being safe and secure

Physical needs for the survival of the physical body

Motivation—Why do you need to understand this?

When counselors try to deal with employment needs before helping the client to overcome barriers to employment such as the more urgent requirements identified by Maslow (to find a place to live, to get over addictions, to get away from a spouse that beats them), they will not succeed. Therefore, an employment counselor must ensure the client is ready to receive employment counseling to deal with employment needs before proceeding on this basis with the client.

Because such urgent needs must be resolved before any employment issues can be tackled, these critical needs are barriers to employment and must be handled on a priority basis by **experts**. Employment counselors need to know when to refer a client to partners who will help them deal with such urgent needs or barriers.

Presentation—How does it work?

The most basic need is the <u>need for the survival of the physical body.</u> Ask yourself what a human body needs to survive and you have identified the needs in this level. Some of the most common ones are food, water, warmth in the winter to avoid freezing, and medicine, in some cases. This is why employment counselors should not proceed with employment action plans if a client does not have a place to live or any money at all to buy food. Such needs must be addressed by the employment counselor through appropriate referrals to partners who help people to deal with them.

Another basic need is the <u>person's need for being safe and secure</u>. If a client is threatened with being beaten or even killed by enemies, or other bullies such as spouses, other students in schools or institutions or the work place, they will not be ready to think clearly about employment needs. As well, if clients are threatened with eviction from their homes, or by divorce/separation from their spouses and they do not want this to happen, they will not be able to deal with employment issues. These are some examples of the kinds of needs that may exist in this level.

The next basic need is <u>the need for love</u>. People who think they are not loved by those who are important to them will be emotionally crippled to the point where they may become mentally ill and unable to cope with daily demands of a job, or school, etc.. This is where people may suffer so much that they start sliding back down the hierarchy of needs and may become a danger to themselves. Suicide is one example of such self-endangerment; or they may eventually lose their livelihood and homes because they are unable to maintain a job or progress at school due to their emotional upset.

It is important to understand that having achieved a certain level in Maslow's Hierarchy of Needs is no guarantee that a person will remain at that level. They may proceed upward or slide back down depending on how successful they are in dealing with the challenges they encounter as they live their lives.

The next level is the person's <u>need for self-esteem</u>. This is a fairly high level in the hierarchy and satisfying this need properly will usually lead to the next level, which is happiness and satisfaction with one's life. Self-esteem comes from the feeling that you are valuable, appreciated, and important and that you do a good job based on what people who matter tell you. But when those who matter (boss, spouse, parents, family, friends, teachers, counselors) do not appreciate you or bother to tell you that you are doing a good job, or worse still that you are not doing a good job, it leads to a slide back down hill to the last level. You wonder if you are loved, and self-doubt starts to grow so that you could slide down … down … unless you gain control over your needs by learning to satisfy them.

The person's need for self-actualization is the ultimate need for a person. Many people who are not at peace with themselves, or feel dissatisfied with their lives, have not satisfied this need. Not too many people do satisfy this need, often because they do not understand the important goals in life. Some think if they have enough money they will be happy. Others think they need to be famous, or beautiful or popular, or outstanding sportsmen or women, yet when they achieve this distinction, they are still not happy. Few people are ready for or understand that an individual's happiness in life depends directly on how happy she or he makes others. Those who are ready for this understanding and achieve it in their lifetime are often called saints.

People who cannot achieve self-actualization after they are rich enough, famous enough and powerful enough are sometimes so unhappy that they become a danger to themselves (suicide) because there is absolutely nothing of interest or importance left to challenge them. This is because they are riveted to themselves, their own feelings, their own happiness, their own life and spare nothing for looking at others' feelings, happiness and lives. Self-actualization depends not only on 'self' but on all those who matter. Learning this lesson early in your life will help you to succeed and reach your ultimate goal in life.

Examples—Show me!

1. A girl who has been living on the street now has a room in a rooming house where she lives and gets some welfare money to help buy food and clothes, but her pimp has beaten her up and threatens to kill her if she doesn't start working again. How can she stop living in fear and proceed to the next level in the hierarchy of needs?

2. The same girl, as in #1 above, now wants to try to get her daughter back from a foster home where the child has been living but she needs to show she is making a serious effort to learn skills in order to get a career that will support them both. When you discuss the client taking training for a job you learn she only has a grade nine education. How do the girl's feelings for her daughter link her into the "need for love" level and why is it important to ensure employment counseling sessions recognize how important the client's daughter is to her plans for success?

Summary and Key Points—What is most important about this issue?

Maslow's Hierarchy of Needs provides important signals about a client's improving or deteriorating lifestyle and behaviors. It is important for an employment counselor to identify the current situation in which the client lives to determine when she or he will be ready to think about and deal with employment related issues. In the meantime, the employment counselor may need to call upon community partners to help the client climb out of the lower levels of the hierarchy in order to overcome barriers to employment.

Self-Test Questions—How well do I understand this?

1. At what level in the hierarchy is a street person addicted to drugs and alcohol and how could an employment counselor help him (remember the community partners …)?

2. How would an employment counselor deal with a person who is crippled and lacking in self-esteem, remembering the balance required in the four quadrants of the medicine wheel and the expertise of the employment counselor?

3. A woman who was a concert pianist has been in an accident and will never play the piano again. She was famous and highly respected. She has returned to the reservation where she was born to live and has come to you to help her get her life together again. She wants to work but does not know what she could do. At what level in Maslow's Hierarchy could this woman be and how would you try to help her?

4

Employment Counseling—The Four Employability Dimensions

Chapter Goal—To plan a balanced approach to achieving employment goals in each employability dimension having regard to the medicine wheel.

Back ground—Important issues about this topic follow.
Important issues in this chapter include the four employability dimensions as a way of grouping employment needs and barriers for assessment. This method also establishes that job maintenance should be reviewed first; career decision making, second; skill enhancement, third; and job search, fourth. The general goal of clients and employment counselors is to establish clients' self-sufficiency, or ability to deal effectively with their own needs, in each of the employability dimensions, as follows:

a.   Job Maintenance

Assess and satisfy client needs to achieve balance in each quadrant of the Medicine Wheel—head, heart, hands, home.

b.   Career Decision Making

Assess and satisfy client needs to achieve balance in each quadrant of the Medicine Wheel—head, heart, hands, home.

c.   Skill Enhancement

Assess and satisfy client needs to achieve balance in each quadrant of the Medicine Wheel—head, heart, hands, home.

d.   Job Search

Assess and satisfy client needs to achieve balance in each quadrant of the Medicine Wheel—head, heart, hands, home.

Motivation—Why do you need to understand this?

Successful employment counseling relies on a systematic approach to discovering employment barriers and needs of clients. The four employability dimensions help to chart a simple path to identifying issues that need attention.

Presentation—How does it work?

The four employability dimensions blend with the four quadrants of the Medicine Wheel in a natural way to promote discovery of needs for resolution so as to achieve balance. Employment counselors use this tool to help uncover and address employment needs and barriers that must be resolved.

The first dimension is **Job Maintenance.** Most barriers to employment exist in this dimension which is why it should be considered before the other dimensions. There is a good possibility that the employment counselor may need to refer clients out to community experts to deal with barriers (such as addictions, or educational upgrading, etc). before going on to the next dimension. On the other hand clients may come to see employment counselors because they have lost jobs due to problems that exist in job maintenance. (Drinking alcohol on the job is most common as well as poor or immature attitudes showing a lack of life skills.) In any case, job maintenance will need to come first when interviewing clients to uncover employment barriers or needs. The employment counselor will determine if an outside referral will be needed.

The first quadrant of the Medicine Wheel is "head" so we will examine all 'job maintenance' issues related to this quadrant first.

The client may establish self-sufficiency under this dimension providing none of the following Job Maintenance issues constitute a barrier to employment or a need that must be satisfied:

Job Maintenance➡ HEAD

- Quitting school, courses, work or being suspended or dismissed
- Mentally challenged (examples: Down Syndrome, product of fetal alcohol/drug abuse syndrome, other)

- Mentally impaired (examples: memory loss/Alzheimer's, drug/alcohol abusers, brain diseases/injuries leaving permanent damage thereby reducing the client's capacity for self-sufficiency/independence, other)
- Lack of creative/lateral thinking
- Illiteracy & innumeracy including linguistic, basic math & computer skills

Job Maintenance ➡ HEART

- Immaturity
- Mentally disturbed (examples: neuroses, psychoses, schizoid, depression, anxiety, other)
- Lack of assertiveness
- Low self-esteem
- Attitude issues

Job Maintenance ➡ HANDS

- Life skills or generic skills including:
  - interpersonal skills
  - communication
  - conflict management
  - self-management
  - time management
  - problem solving
  - goal setting
  - organizing
  - adapting
  - self-confidence
  - fiscal management
  - work habits
  - personal hygiene
  - punctuality

- No parenting skills (and is a parent)
- Criminal activities
- Self-identified physical disabilities

Job Maintenance ➡ HOME

- Poor values/belief systems
- Victims of violence
- Previously institutionalized (hospitalized, incarcerated)

It is important that if a case manager suspects there may be problems that may constitute barriers in this dimension, the client is referred out to a specialist for assessment and if necessary, treatment.

Under no circumstances are case managers to exceed their level of competence in this dimension.

The second dimension is **Career Decision Making**. This dimension requires the employment counselor to lead the client on a journey of self-examination in the four areas of the Medicine Wheel to ascertain strengths and weaknesses in the four quadrants: 'head/intelligence', 'heart/emotions', 'hands/physical' and 'home/spiritual'.

This self examination will determine the level of education/knowledge that might be needed by clients, interests and desires of clients, abilities and talents they possess compared to the skills they would need. Finally, the values and beliefs possessed by clients impact on the kind of jobs they would be comfortable in doing. Employment counselors should assist clients in scanning the local labor market to assess the demand for skills by employers in the community where clients intend to work. This will help them realize what their chances for finding work will be.

Clients may establish self-sufficiency under this dimension providing none of the following Career Decision Making issues constitute unsatisfied needs identified in an interview under this dimension:

Career Decision Making➡ HEAD

- Knowledge of local labor market conditions especially those concerning demand occupations
- Education level

Career Decision Making➡ HEART

- Awareness of own interests/aptitudes
- Research on occupations of interest
- Establish criteria (working conditions, wages, benefits, security, skills needed, job satisfaction, etc.) for making occupational choices
- Establish priorities in occupational choices
- Select a few occupational alternatives
- The chosen occupation builds self-esteem

Career Decision Making➡ HANDS

- Existing skills are valuable in the new occupation
- Clients have ability or talent to learn new skills

Career Decision Making➡ HOME

- Existing experience is valuable in the new occupation
- Clients' belief and value systems are not compromised by prospective career

The third employability dimension is **Skill Enhancement**, where clients will take appropriate training to acquire the skills needed in the occupation of his/her choice. Some issues that are important when choosing training include the quality and cost of the training and resulting certification.

Clients may establish self-sufficiency under this dimension providing none of the following Skill Enhancement issues constitute unsatisfied needs identified in an interview:

Skill Enhancement ➡ HEAD

- Inadequate educational prerequisites to take occupational training

- Inadequate ability to acquire education to meet occupational requirements and or those barriers listed under job maintenance

- Inadequate planning to acquire the training and/or work experience to achieve occupational goals

- Inadequate access to technical/professional knowledge to learn or perform certain occupations

Skill Enhancement ➡ HEART

- Lack of appreciation of the commitment needed to accomplish education and training to become successful

- Lack of commitment to persevere in achieving occupational goal

- Other interests take precedence

Skill Enhancement ➡ HANDS

- Client does not have ability or talent to acquire necessary skills

- Client suffers some impairment that interferes with his/her ability to perform the skill or to continue to learn the skill

Skill Enhancement ➡ HOME

- Clients' "baggage" such as poorly arranged personal life interfere with their ability to achieve good results or even to continue in the training;

The fourth employability dimension is **Job Search.** Clients require supervision and mentoring to perform effective job search. Some employers will need incentives such a wage subsidy program to hire clients if they are inexperienced. Employment counselors are expected to train clients on how job search is done in certain occupations and create action plans with them that take such approaches into consideration.

The client may establish self-sufficiency under this dimension providing none of the following <u>Job Search</u> issues constitute unsatisfied needs identified in an interview under this dimension:

Job Search ➡ HEAD

- Clients may or may not understand how to look for work in their occupation
- Clients know how to create job search tools (resumes, portfolios, etc.)
- Clients understand how to keep job search records and why they are important
- Clients know where there are good opportunities for work in their chosen occupation
- Clients know relevant labor market information about their occupation (job profile)

Job Search ➡ HEART

- Clients are genuinely committed to finding work (or are they only going out to find work because a social worker said they will not be paid unless they do so)
- Clients have a good, positive attitudes about job search (they do not go out thinking they are never going to be hired because they are not good enough)
- Clients put aside emotional problems to concentrate on job search

Job Search ➡ HANDS

- Clients are able to communicate effectively in person, by phone and in writing
- Clients are able to develop effective networks to help in their job search
- Clients are able to market themselves to employers
- Clients have no limiting physical or mental problems that interfere with their efforts to find work

Job Search ➡ HOME

- Clients do not let "baggage" interfere with their efforts to find work
- Clients arrange their personal life to allow them the freedom to seek work and to accept a job if it is offered

Examples—Show me!

1. A client who has been severely burned in his lower body comes to see you and it is obvious he has a bad limp. Through a discussion of his needs under the "hands/physical" portion of the Medicine Wheel you discover that the client does not consider himself handicapped in any way. He says he is a truck driver who needs some information technology training in order to keep his job as a truck driver with his current employer.

2. The trucks the client in number 1 is expected to drive now have the latest computers on board to regulate everything from the temperature of the produce he transports to the air in the tires. His current employer says he will pay half the cost of training for this client. The first employment issue we have discovered is under job maintenance: if the client wants to remain employed in his job with this employer, he needs training in information technology. The client has established a legitimate need in this dimension and we can now work together to plan a solution with him. This client is <u>not</u> considered a person with a disability because he has not identified himself as being someone who has special needs in this regard. Therefore, we consider him as a regular client in all ways, including the funding sources we would use to pay for his interventions.

3. A twenty-one year old youth comes to see a counselor saying he has successfully graduated from a water treatment course with a recognized college but has been unable to find a job in any Aboriginal communities because they have no money to hire someone without experience. It is the same story for non-Aboriginal communities and perhaps even worse because, according to the youth, there seems to be an element of prejudice keeping him out of the running for well-paying positions. The counselor determines that the client has no needs under job maintenance, career decision making or skill enhancement, only under job search. After discussing the client's job search methods the counselor feels this youth has been doing a proper job search and is a candidate for targeted wage subsidy. A new job search plan is created whereby the youth not only approaches desirable potential employers, but uses newly learned self-marketing techniques to land a good job.

4. A 50-year old widow who lived all her life on the reserve comes to see the employment counselor. She is a severe diabetic and in deteriorating

health. She has no income except social service allowance that is not enough to pay for her daily needs because of the extra medication she requires that is not covered by the government health care coverage she now has. She says if she could get a part-time job she could pay for the additional medication she needs and become healthier. Besides, she is tired of living on the reserve and needs to be in the city where doctors and jobs are available. She only has grade four education but she wants to be a licensed practical nurse in a hospital where she can work with doctors and nurses. The counselor determines that this client has barriers to employment that include lack of education under the head/intellectual part of the Medicine Wheel, and under the hand/physical section where she has poor health. However, her courage under the heart/emotional quadrant and her spiritual strength to carry on, under the home/spiritual quadrant of the Medicine Wheel, will help her to overcome many obstacles that would stop a weaker person. The employment counselor decides she is a good risk for training because she is committed to survival. The career choice will be tested to see if this is really what she wants to do or if there are other occupations that might be better suited to her needs. Since the client has admitted she has some issues with diabetes she may be referred to partners who offer in-depth services to persons with disabilities. The <u>best partners in this area would be those who deal on an exclusive basis with persons who have disabilities and they would</u>:

a.   Ensure her diabetes is under control.

b.   Help her to look after her needs for housing in the city where she proposes to live (ensuring there are no barriers to successful plans for employment).

c.   Help her to choose an appropriate career given her age, health, interests, etc..

d.   Help her to create and carry out an action plan that includes attention to her medical requirements under the care of a doctor; attention to her educational upgrading requirements under the supervision of an educational institution; attention to skills training under the supervision of an accredited training institution; and attention to job search.

e.   Assist in paying for the costs of all of these interventions.

Summary and Key Points—What is most important about this issue?

The order of consideration of issues set out by the four employability dimensions ensures a systematic approach to dealing with barriers to employment and employment needs. Barriers to employment often exist because the client is stuck in a lower echelon of Maslow's Hierarchy of Needs. On this basis, job maintenance is always reviewed first because most barriers to employment exist in this dimension and need to be removed before employment needs can be addressed.

The four employability dimensions are Job Maintenance, Career Decision Making, Skill Enhancement, and Job Search. Each one of the four employability dimensions is examined through the prism of the four quadrants of the Medicine Wheel. In other words, when we are exploring the client's barriers and needs under job maintenance, we explore using head, heart, hands and home as our guide, and when the appropriate time comes, we go on to career decision making, skill enhancement and job search where we again explore using head, heart, hands and home as the guide. This is not all done in one interview. Instead such discussion occurs as the client progresses through his/her action plan and may takes many months before the employment counseling sessions are completed and the client finds suitable work.

This formula ensures that employment counseling is carried out in a systematic way in order to help **the client** recognize barriers to employment that need resolution before dealing with employment needs. This approach also relies on **the client** creating an action plan to achieve the desired employment goal with the assistance and in agreement with the employment counselor.

Self-Test Questions—How well do I understand this?

1. A 45-year old client comes in to see an employment counselor after losing his job. He hurt his knees and back and can no longer do laboring work. He has a grade five education and wants training to be a truck driver. What employability dimension should be considered first, second and third?

2. What barriers to employment exist and what partners might help the client in #1 to deal with his barriers?

3. What self examination must this man undertake when deciding on a career?

4. What external scan of the labor market would be important for this client to do before choosing a career as a truck driver?

5

Locus of Control & Empowerment

Chapter Goal—To achieve balance in exercising control over those things within our power, and to enable others to assume control over problems that they own.

Background—Important issues about this topic follow.
Important issues to understand are that most people do not want to be blamed when something goes wrong, but avoiding ownership of a problem is also avoiding taking on the power to fix it. Yet, whoever is to blame, is the one who must do something to correct the problem and therefore has the power to do this. Everyone else just waits until someone does something because they are "not responsible." Are you a "waiter" because nothing is ever your fault? If so, you are disempowered and rely on others to use their power to make things happen.

Motivation—Why do you need to understand this?

Some employment counselors are just as disempowered as their clients. Until they learn how to take control of their own destiny, they will not be very effective in helping their clients learn how to empower themselves.

Presentation—How does it work?

If you or your client's first response to challenges is "I can't" or "it won't work ..." or "no way!" or "it won't happen ..." then you are disempowered and have no control over the things happening to you in your life. You have made your main job in your life to wait for miracles like winning the lottery, or for someone to give you something for nothing, or for the fairy godmother to grant a wish … but if the main way you live your life right now is to WAIT for something good to happen to you, then you are a "waiter" and your life is frustrating because it is tossed like a leaf in the wind by forces that you do not even try to control. You tell yourself and others that you "can't." You may just keep on waiting for the rest of your life. As a waiter and employment counselor, you may be able to motivate your client to do the things you suggest in order to achieve an employment goal even though that person is a waiter too. But the locus of control in your life is external as you have given it away to others and wait for something good to happen to you.

Such people blame others or circumstances for their problems. This raises the question of <u>who owns the problem?</u> Blaming others for their unhappiness is easy and allows them to lean back and do nothing. They wait until those people stop or start doing what they desire. They make others responsible for the problem because they themselves are not at fault! If only they could understand that until they own the problem, they can do nothing about it except wait for whoever they blame for the difficulty to do something about it.

If they take back the locus of control and make it internal to themselves, then they assume control of their destiny by making the best possible choices in challenges facing them. This does not automatically ensure they will succeed, but it ensures they will not wait like victims for the wolf to come to them.

Owning our problems is a giant step toward <u>growing up and taking responsibility for ourselves</u>. If we shoulder the blame for our problems, we can finally line up some choices to lead us away from the rut in which we have been "waiting."

Yet, it is important to understand **who owns the problem**. Some aggressive types of people take control of all problems whether or not they own the problem. These people certainly have an internal locus of control and are usually considered powerful. They take control to get what they want, manipulating everything to their advantage. They come across as being "bossy." This can be disruptive for those who do own the problem and try to control it. They will find interference at every turn and may wind up with bad results due to choices others have made for them.

Therefore, when determining if the locus of control is internal or external, the most important issue to resolve is "WHO OWNS THE PROBLEM?" It is the owners of the problem, who should act to resolve it and not let others do it for them. Owning the problem means they may act on their own behalf and empower themselves to realize their goals.

Employment counselors have two main duties in helping clients to empower themselves:

- To encourage clients to make choices thereby empowering them to achieve their goals; and

- To present an array of appropriate choices leading to desired goals from which the client may choose.

When clients explore issues using the Medicine Wheel, they are more likely to identify imbalances in their lives and to own the problems that lead to these imbalances. They are also more likely to participate in action planning and in carrying out the plans, giving them ownership of their own problems. This is how counselors may empower their clients, instilling an internal locus of control.

Locus of Control➤ HEAD

- Who is responsible for getting an appropriate education? It is the person who owns the problem, the one who needs the education.

Locus of Control➤ HEART

- Who needs to commit to achieve desirable employment goals? It is the person who owns the problem, the one who wants to achieve such goals.

Locus of Control➤ HANDS

- Who needs to develop skills and abilities to perform desired employment? It is the person who owns the problem, the one who needs these skills and abilities to perform work in the chose occupation.

Locus of Control➤ HOME

- Who needs to use values, beliefs, support, and experiences to help achieve success? It is the one who owns the problem who needs to draw on this personal support to succeed.

Employment counselors may elect to share power with their clients but must ensure they are not giving up their authority at the same time. Such power sharing needs to be done carefully in situations where there is a great deal of mutual trust and respect between the employment counselor and the client. The following are some rules for such power sharing which are worthwhile in attempting to empower clients to deal with their employment issues.

1. We will only share power with people we trust.

2. We get the behavior we expect. If we do not trust, people will not behave in a trustworthy way, but by trusting we elicit trustworthy behavior.

3. When we protect people and do things for them, they do not become responsible for themselves but they become powerless and dependent. Therefore, we need to allow people to be responsible for themselves.

4. Responsible decision making is learned, but usually not without mistakes. Mistakes are learning opportunities and a sign of growth, not failure. People must not be protected from their mistakes.

5. Just the good intentions of organizational leaders do not ensure a well-designed agency. Appropriate organizational design where power sharing is spread out leads to success, whereas coercion and oppression with centralized power leads to failure.

6. For most organizations, clients are treated in the same way that the organization's workers are treated.

7. Counselors who feel powerless are seldom able to keep clients from also feeling powerless. Therefore, it is imperative that counselors are themselves empowered.

Four undesirable consequences of failure to empower clients are:

1. Clients will stay dependent on service agencies because they will not be able to find other solutions.

2. Clients will seem to be lazy, disrespectful, untrustworthy, irresponsible and dependent on others for their well being.

3. Clients will not cooperate with counselors.

4. Clients will be unduly competitive wanting to "win" at any cost.

<u>If you have trouble getting along with co-workers look at yourself and ask why this is the case.</u> (It could be the reason why you have trouble being a good counselor.)

Examples—Show me!

1. *"The car broke down so I won't be in to work on time."* The person's choice of words shows he/she blames the car for breaking down so there may be an external locus of control. They may not accept responsibility for the break down of the car even though the maintenance and repair of the car is their problem. Instead they blame poor luck or the car is a lemon.

2. *"They took away my driver's license so I can't get a job."* Based on the person's choice of words, there seems to be an external locus of control with "they" being to blame for the loss of a license and the client's inability to find work. Everything is "their" fault and the client must now wait until he gets his license back so s/he can look for work.

3. *"My employment counselor refused to train me so I can't get a job."* The person seems to have an external locus of control and blames the employment counselor for his/her inability to find work.

4. *"I believe in mind over matter."* The person seems to have an internal locus of control and believes circumstances can be controlled by his/her mind.

5. *"I am a healer and can cure you of your disease through the power of my mind."* The person seems to have an internal locus of control and uses it to help others.

6. *"I am a hypnotist and can control other people's minds when people agree to hypnosis."* The person seems to have an *internal* locus of control and uses it to hypnotize others when they agree to such action.

Summary and Key Points—What is most important about this issue?

• Locus of control refers to how much control clients feel they have over what happens to them. Those with an internal locus of control feel things happen because of their own efforts, while those with external locus of control feel they have little or no control over what happens to them.

Self-Test Questions—How well do I understand this?

Is the locus of control internal or external in these situations and why do you think so?

1. Parent speaking to a neighbor: "If you have a problem with my teenaged son, speak to me, not to him!"

2. Teenager in a car accident: "I should never have gone out tonight. I knew it was New Year's Eve and there would be drunk drivers on the road."

3. A gambler who just won a jackpot: "I just kept putting loonies into the slot machine until I made it pay off."

4. Client in an employment centre: "I told her I wanted another counselor because I did not like her!"

6

Lateral Thinking

Chapter Goal—To achieve balance in thinking approaches means people must use both lateral and vertical thinking as complementary processes to solve problems.

Background—Important issues about this topic follow.
Important issues to understand are that lateral thinking ensures many options and ideas are included and explored *outside* of the predictable, logical paths. Vertical thinking ensures the chosen solution satisfies the needs or criteria, and that the solution is successfully implemented and evaluated through a *step-by-step* action plan. (This is akin to the scientific method.)

Motivation—Why do you need to understand this?

Employment counselors must lead clients to think laterally in order to generate innovative solutions to their employment problems. On the other hand they must also help the client to think vertically in order to create the steps in an action plan leading to the client's solution/employment goal.

Presentation—How does it work?

A basic understanding of human thinking patterns helps employment counselors to impart information to clients and to assist them in solving their employment issues. <u>The following is important to remember about how the mind works:</u>

1. Clients' experience and other attributes brought from the home quadrant of the Medicine Wheel (values, beliefs, assumptions) influence thinking patterns. They use this home background to recognize similar situations automatically comparing what they now face to what they did in the past and make decisions using the old, established thinking pat-

terns. It does not matter if a pattern is right or wrong, as long as it is distinct and clear-cut. Instincts such as hunger or thirst are not thinking patterns.

2. The mind's unfamiliarity/inexperience regarding the importance of context around an issue has a serious impact on any solutions being considered in one's mind. Here is an example of the impact of context or the conditions surrounding an issue under consideration: drop a block of wood while standing on the ground and it falls; but under water it rises, while in outer space it floats. A person brings personal context from his home quadrant on the Medicine Wheel although other quadrants also could bring forth conditions (e.g. disabilities from the hands quadrant, mental slowness from the head quadrant, etc.).

3. In my experience, teachers sometimes said "wrinkles" were formed in our brains as we learned something new. This is a good illustration. Another image of learning is when hot water falls a drop at a time onto a smooth surface of Jell-O, scoring its surface. Similarly, new learning leaves memory traces in the brain.

4. It is important to impart new knowledge at a rate that is comfortable to the learner because our minds have limited attention spans. We are overwhelmed when we must think of more than one idea at a time and the result of bombarding the mind with too much at one time is comparable to pouring lots of hot water onto the Jell-O, resulting in a meltdown.

5. Although the mind can choose information it needs, or reject it, or combine it with other information or separate information from other information as it pleases, the information must make sense as soon as the mind receives it. The information cannot be stored in the mind and retrieved later on because if it is not understood it will be deemed gibberish. There will be no "storage links" which we can use to find it again. Therefore, such information will either not be understood or its impact will not be understood. Once again, a person's past experience provides critical links to anchor new learning in the mind. When there is no past experience of any sort, new learning will not occur easily until some experience accompanies it. This underscores the importance of hands-on learning or even contrived learning situations through vicarious experiences or simulations.

6. Some experiential learning is so intense that it can alter the state of the client in the quadrants of the Medicine Wheel. An example is where the values and beliefs in the Home quadrant change as a result of a significant emotional event where the mind experiences trauma that upsets its equilibrium. This kind of learning can leave emotional scarring that would need attention to make the person mentally healthy again. Other experiential learning of a less intense nature comes when we have a sudden insight and might say "Aha!" Such insights open doors to whole new fields of learning for the mind allowing it to recognize and store knowledge it would have previously rejected.

Differences Between Lateral & Vertical Thinking

Lateral	Vertical
• Stimulating	• Established and stable
• May skip from one issue to another	• Moves in an orderly way, no skipping
• Brings about re-patterning, new patterns	• Follows set patterns
• May move and change directions	• Moves only if there is a direction in which to move
• Intuitive, relies on gut feelings	• Relies on logic
• Is not continuous and does not depend on what went before or comes after	• Analytical and sequential
• Correctness is not important	• Must be correct at every step or blocks will stop process
• Everything is possible, no negatives	• All things irrelevant are excluded
• Mistakes are welcomed	• Mistakes are shunned
• Labels, classifications are unimportant	• Labels, classifications are important
• All paths are open	• Explore only most likely paths
• Work on all probabilities	• Work to an exact solution only and end there
• Inductive reasoning	• Deductive reasoning

There are some proven ways to promote lateral thinking, as the following list illustrates:

1. **Generating alternatives** (similar to brainstorming) for new ways of looking at things, new patterns and re-patterning.

2. **Asking "why"** to reassemble information and change established patterns. A trap to watch out for is sowing too much doubt that a good decision is not possible. Asking "why" repeatedly is the classic approach to "issue analysis" and helps to get to the root causes of barriers blocking.

3. **Suspending judgment** even when ideas seem wrong allows the idea to survive long enough to breed other ideas, and it tests the "context" (remember the block of wood falling on the ground, floating upwards under water and floating in space after it has been dropped) to see if it will lead to something promising.

4. **Prioritizing** helps to distinguish the importance of an idea to see if it is a "dominant idea" that leads to a new way of looking at things (re-patterning) or, it can be a "crucial factor" which must be considered no matter which way we look at things. Crucial factors should be carefully reviewed to ensure they are "crucial" because these factors usually have a way of limiting options. (Example: a dominant idea is to give a patient a blood transfusion to survive, but if the person's religion—a crucial factor—does not allow for this, then the options are limited as far as blood transfusions are concerned.)

5. **Fractioning** is a method of breaking down an issue into its component parts to stimulate restructuring them in a new way. A classic example of this is when the path clients take to receive employment service continues to be reviewed and changed to respond to clients' needs and to streamline service.

6. **Reversing** is looking at things from back to front or upside down to gain a new perspective. Rarely is the reverse point of view correct but it can point out critical points impacting on the problem to be solved. A good way to use this approach is to work backwards from a vision or a goal to be achieved to see where it leads.

7. **Brainstorming** uses two main features to list options: stimulating the participants to contribute, and suspending judgment in an informal setting where all ideas are accepted. The options generated this way need to be reviewed and rated in some way. Suggested rating could be:

   • Directly useful

   • Interesting approach

- Examine further
- Discard

8. **Analogies and attention points** are ways to get ideas moving by focusing on different aspects of the problem and making comparisons with other situations that seem similar.

Examples—Show me!

1. The employment counselor identified two barriers to employment facing the client in the job maintenance dimension: alcohol addiction and lack of education (grade four). The employment counselor suggested that the client's addiction to alcohol was a priority for intervention (vertical thinking) because the client needed to be lucid and capable of making responsible decisions without the pressure of the alcohol addiction clouding his mind. After the addiction was under control, the client could choose a career (lateral thinking)and get the education needed to perform the job (vertical thinking).

2. The administrative assistant led a brainstorm session to list options for spending $100 in lottery winnings by office staff (lateral thinking). A small water fountain for the reception area was the popular choice and two people were assigned to shop for the best deal in terms of appearance, price and size (vertical thinking).

3. The family shared their suggestions for a vacation destination (lateral thinking). Then they set up criteria that needed to be met in choosing the vacation spot and evaluated each of the suggestions using these criteria to select the best option (vertical thinking).

Summary and Key Points—What is most important about this issue?

Employment counselors use lateral and vertical thinking in carrying out their responsibilities. After the client identifies the imbalance problem he/she is experiencing by using the Medicine Wheel, the employment counselor works with the client using lateral thinking to generate an array of solutions that might meet the client's needs from which the client may choose. After agreeing on the appropriateness of the solution, the employment counselor will help the client create an action plan that shows how the client's goal will be achieved step-by-step. This orderly progression towards the client's goal uses vertical thinking like a set of stairs where each step helps to get closer to the goal.

Self-Test Questions—How well do I understand this?

1. An exercise encourages people to make brainstorm suggestions according to the color of the hat they wear. For instance if they wear a black hat their suggestions will always be negative, and if they wear red, their suggestions will be emotional, etc.. Is this lateral or vertical thinking and why?

2. Why is an action plan a good example of vertical thinking?

3. When a person keeps asking "why" to analyze a problem, is this an example of vertical or lateral thinking (example: **Why** is the client unemployed? He has no job. **Why** does the client have no job? He has no skills. **Why** does the client have no skills? He has no training. **Why** does the client have no training? He does not have enough education. **Why** does the client not have enough education? He quit school. **Why** did the client quit school? He became addicted to alcohol and got into trouble with the law … etc.)?

7

The Grieving Cycle

Chapter Goal—To help client achieve balance after experiencing a loss in their lives.

Background—Important issues about this topic follow.
Important issues include a better understanding of how interactions with clients may be influenced by behaviors resulting from grief due to the death of a loved one or other sudden adverse change. While some clients may not think they have been adversely impacted by their experience, in reality, they may be going through a grieving cycle that needs to be dealt with before properly considering employment issues.

Motivation—Why do you need to understand this?

Just as people who are stuck in the lower rungs of Maslow's Hierarchy of Needs are not prepared to deal with less critical issues facing them until the most threatening ones are satisfied, grieving in its various stages may set up barriers to dealing with employment problems. Employment counselors need to recognize these barriers and help clients overcome them. Most often outside partners may be requested to assist clients to deal with their grief so they may prepare to deal with employment issues. However, employment counselors need to understand that even referring a client to outside partners may be premature if the client is still in shock from the trauma of the tragedy. In such cases, after ensuring the client has an adequate support system around him or her, it might be best to delay any further activity around employment issues until the client is ready to proceed. If clients are caught up in a grieving cycle, an employment counselor will need to understand where they are in that cycle to look for signs of the emotions the client is experiencing at that time in order to determine what employment-related interventions might be appropriate, if any.

Presentation—How does it work?

The grieving cycle is experienced to a greater or lesser degree by anyone who has suffered a loss. These losses may include deaths of loved ones, other personal tragedies such as divorces, or less shocking occurrences including financial problems, failures at school or work, or even changes in daily routines that are difficult to accept. From the perspective of an employment counselor, we will consider the impact of losing a job as the factor generating the client's grief.

For our purposes, the heart quadrant on the Medicine Wheel, where emotions are raw and irritated, is out of balance and may adversely impact all of the other quadrants. People may become physically ill (hands), their sense of values and beliefs may be shaken up (home), and their ability to reason may be compromised for a period of time (head). For this reason it is important to recognize the stage of grief being experienced by the client to ensure clients are given proper consideration for the barriers they face at this time. Professor Norman Amundsen of University of British Columbia has authored articles on how job loss results in a grieving cycle such as the one described by Doctor Elizabeth Kubler-Ross, that bereaved people experience. (See the bibliography for more information on resources available on this issue.) According to Amundsen, grief over job loss, like other personal losses, may give rise to the following emotions and behaviors:

1. Shock and anger (first negative reactions to loss)

2. Worried, sad (thinking about loss)

3. Determined, on top of things (beginning to accept loss)

4. Hopeful, optimistic, proud (regrouping inner resources and thinking about life after the loss)

5. Pressured, discouraged, afraid, angry, desperate (reactions to stress associated with experiencing life after the loss)

6. Apathetic (protecting self from experiencing more hurt)

7. Feeling worthless, isolated, lonely, drifting (reliving the guilt feelings associated with the loss)

8. Re-employment or deciding to retire from the labor market (finding peace of mind allowing a person to move on).

Knowing these phases allows counselors to understand their client's behavior and how to help them. In order to assess a client's readiness to properly consider employment issues, counselors could follow this approach:

- Observe the client's behavior

- Decide what emotions the client is expressing through this behavior

- Compare the emotions expressed by the client to those listed in steps 1 through 7 of the grieving cycle

- Determine what phase of the grieving cycle the client is now experiencing in order to anticipate the degree to which the client is prepared to deal with employment issues

Note: In extreme cases job loss by itself may have a serious impact on the client or it may only be one of a series of problems being faced by a client. Counselors must be able to recognize the need for referral to specialists if necessary. Employment counselors must restrict themselves to dealing with employment issues and arrange for appropriate referrals when the client is not yet ready to deal with employment considerations.

Examples—Show me!

1. A client who was ready to begin a training course in two weeks calls to say his four-year-old son was killed when he backed over him in his car. He can barely speak because he is so grief stricken. His wife comes on the phone and says she will come in to see the counselor on her husband's behalf in a few days to postpone the training course. The employment counselor reviews later start dates for the course and makes a note of them to share with the client's wife. In the meantime, the client's seat in the course is cancelled. When the wife comes in the new possible start dates for the course are shared with her and names of partners who deal in grief counseling are also shared with a recommendation that both she and her husband go to see them. The wife says the husband is under the supervision of his doctor for the time being. Satisfied that the client will return to the employment centre when he is ready, the employment counselor puts the file away with a "bring-forward" date of six months later for follow-up contact with the client.

2. A 50-year-old client lost his job where he had worked for 21 years with the result that he lost all of his accumulated pension benefits even

though he would be paid out a lump sum. During the interview with the employment counselor, the client seems confused and emotional. He has difficulty speaking about his job loss and keeps muttering "I don't know what I am going to do now! I am too old! I do not have any training! I was going to retire in 10 years ... I don't know what I am going to do ..." The counselor decides that the client is still in shock over his job loss and needs some time to let it sink in before they discuss future employment possibilities. The client seems to be firmly facing the past and locked into it so he needs some time to be able to turn around and face the future. The employment counselor suggests the client may want to talk to his family doctor about how he is feeling and also, if the client goes to church, to his pastor. The employment counselor also gives the man some cards with contacts for persons who are looking for work who are over 45 years old.

3. In the meantime, the employment counselor listens to the client as he explains why the employer was unfair and only let him go to avoid paying a pension. As he speaks, it is clear that the client is becoming angry over his job loss and decides he will look into wrongful dismissal. He leaves the employment counselor saying he is going to see a lawyer. The employment counselor gives him a card and asks him to come back when he is ready to look at other employment options.

Summary and Key Points—What is most important about this issue?

Clients may not be ready to deal with employment issues until they overcome barriers arising from personal tragedy or adverse change. Employment counselors must be aware of the behaviors exhibited by the client that establish the client is not ready for employment counseling and refer the client to appropriate partners for help to overcome such obstacles.

Self-Test Questions—How well do I understand this?

What should the employment counselor do when:

1. A client says he is through looking for work because he will never find any. He is just "not good enough" for any employers. When the employment counselor asks the client what he will do if he is no longer looking for work, the client answers, "Nothing."

2. A client brags that she has a wonderful job search technique and shows her forms. She is bubbly and confident saying she enjoys interviews with employers. She is almost certain she will be offered a job in the next few weeks.

3. A client says she feels like slapping some of the employers she has spoken with because they only smile and shake their heads at her, saying she is not right for them. The employment counselor sees the client is enraged, clenching her teeth and fists as she tries to control her anger and impatience at her lack of success.

8

Motivation & Resistance

Chapter Goal—To achieve spiritual balance when one appreciates the profound value of "serenity" as expressed in the following prayer:

God, grant me
The serenity to accept the things I cannot change
Courage to change the things I can, and
Wisdom to know the difference
-By Reinhold Niebuhr

Background—Important issues about this topic follow.
Important issues to understand are that motivation and resistance are inextricably linked to locus of control in that this prayer underlines the issue of who owns the problem? Alcoholics anonymous use this prayer because it is important for people living with alcoholics as well as the alcoholics themselves to know who owns the problem. Alcoholics often blame others for making them into drunkards and people living with alcoholics often accept that blame and enable them to continue in their destructive lifestyle. Being wise enough to know "who owns the problem" is the first step to empowerment and to make positive changes.

Motivation—Why do you need to understand this?

The most important goal of an employment counseling relationship with a client is to empower him/her to change the things they can, for the better. Therefore, it is important for both the employment counselor and the client to understand what things are within their locus of control (within their power) to change. In this regard, it is imperative to know who owns the problem because it is that person who is the only one with control/power to make the changes.

Presentation—How does it work?

Voluntarily changing things is not easy. It is human nature to resist change so expecting employment counselors to motivate and lead clients to make changes in an orderly fashion is a challenge.

Business guru, Tom Peters, devised a most revealing "change exercise." It has often been used to illustrate the impact of change. It is done by pairs of partners facing each other and following simple commands to change their appearance while observing the reactions of their partners to the changes being made. Although the exercise has been conducted in many ways, the scenario yielding the highest impact begins with an intense scrutiny of the partner facing you for about thirty seconds, which seems like an eternity when there is total silence. Below is a summary of <u>behaviors </u>the participants observed and some that they admitted to experiencing during the course of the exercise. Key words describing feelings and behaviors are highlighted.

1. When asked to take note of their partner's appearance, participants experienced **discomfort** in studying their partner too closely and in being examined by their partner. They showed **worry** about what they might be asked to do.

2. When asked to change five things about their appearance, participants were **reluctant** to do so and when they did, they usually **looked for easy ways to change** so they took off watches, rings, glasses and other easy to remove items to meet the requirement of changing five things about their appearance.

3. When asked to change a further five things about their appearance participants expressed **frustration and resistance**, saying this was becoming a "strip show." The new demands for change were more **aggravating** because now it was no longer easy to remove articles of clothing without risking embarrassment. Nevertheless, few considered any other option than to take things off … thereby **equating change to loss**.

4. When asked yet again to change a further five things about their appearance, the **resistance hardened** in many and they were ready to quit the exercise. However, with others, some real thinking went on at this point about how to accomplish change without stripping naked. (This is

where it was easy to see who was now switching to positive, lateral, or creative thinking to solve a problem. Those who continued in the **negative mode** were **frustrated** and ready to **admit defeat** while others who thought laterally **conceived of new approaches** to meet the change requirement.)

5. It is only after participants were **pushed to their limit of tolerance in meeting change demands** that they freely engaged in **putting things on (positive mode)** that they did not have on before (paper hats, pens in pockets, etc.) or adding things to their appearance. Thus, they found that **change did not mean loss unless they wanted it to mean that** and **they could choose to make it mean "gain" instead.**

6. It was also at this point that some participants conceived of the notion of exchanging things with their partner and **not working alone, but in partnership, to achieve change.** This made the goals of the exercise easier to achieve.

7. At this point, the facilitator purposely ignored the group for a long period of time, until the group decided perhaps the exercise was over … and **they were uncomfortable in their changed state.** As they did not want to remain this way they hurriedly put on all the items they had previously removed and sat back down, relaxing in **the comfort of their previous state**.

8. This illustrated that **change is uncomfortable** and **needs to be facilitated**. It also showed that **participants in change mode try to revert to the comfort of their previous state** regardless of how dangerous or unsuitable their old position had been.

This exercise demonstrates what counselors should expect when they must lead the change the client wants to achieve. Below are the main duties of counselors in leading change for clients:

1. <u>**Motivating**</u> the client to change is critical and means clients should be encouraged to envision or dream about goals that would be achieved through change. Some clients might need to be led through an exploration of what the future would be if they do not achieve the change they envision.

2. <u>**Overcoming resistance**</u> to change by helping the client to view change as gaining access to their goals, (not a loss) and clearly presenting the

positive aspects of change as seen in their vision or dream and by showing the client how change can be implemented with help through partnerships with the counselor and with other experts and service providers in the community.

3. **Leading the change** during the counseling relationship through case management.

Change usually arises from events occurring in one's environment that may precipitate sudden new needs for the client or from a need to adapt voluntarily to achieve goals. In both cases, clients need to adapt to change.

Some **changes may be involuntary**, such as crippling accidents, death of loved ones, etc. while **others may be voluntary** such as when clients decide to work toward goals they have set for themselves. As was seen in the analysis of the change exercise, how clients cope with change will ultimately determine how successful they are at adapting.

The principles of the Medicine Wheel and the "4-H" approach to counseling help us to understand how the client might deal with change and what we can do to assist them.

HEAD/Intellectual—client's level of knowledge (education & training) influences how the client copes with change;

HEART/Emotional—client's emotions influence how the client copes with change;

HANDS/Physical—client's health and/or physical environment influences how the client copes with change; and

HOME/Spiritual—client's values and beliefs acquired from his/her upbringing influence how the client deals with change. In addition, the level of support the client can expect from his family or community will affect how the client copes with change.

Another important variable impacting change is whether the change is involuntary or voluntary. This impacts on how well the client will adapt to the change.

Examples—Show me!

1. A teenager moves to a new city leaving behind all of his friends. He did not want to move and he is quite unhappy. For a month or two he relives his loss and talks about his old set of friends and how the old school was better. However, within three months he joins the school soccer club and band (adding things to his plate to keep him busy and making new friends). He talks less and less about his old friends and school and accepts the change in his life.

2. A client finds a new job that pays better than her old one but she misses her friends from her last job. At first, she feels the change resulted in a loss of friends because she is lonely and struggling to make friends with the new staff but they are all much older than she. They have families and children so she has little in common with them. One day, one of the men on staff invites her to attend a church group meeting where he is an aide. Even though she seldom goes to church, she accepts. Not only does she form a whole new circle of youthful friends, but she brings many of the friends she had from her old job to the church as well. She also meets many other volunteers in the networks in which she participates.

Summary and Key Points—What is most important about this issue?

Employment counseling is an exercise led by a counselor to help a client achieve a voluntary, desirable change in their employment status. Change will often be influenced by the systems the client brings from home and counselors should be on the look out for behaviors that show the client is resisting the change. This is when the counselor will need to lead the change and motivate the client to exercise control over the issues he/she can control to bring progress toward the desired goal.

The most important "lucky learning lesson" the client can learn from the counselor is that she or he is "lucky" to own their problem because <u>only the owner of the problem can implement the changes needed to fix it!</u> How one adjusts to change often depends on how positive one is to new challenges.

Self-Test Questions—How well do I understand this?

1. The client says: "I can't find a good job that pays enough money to support my wife and three kids. I have looked for weeks and weeks and there is nothing I can do. I need to register here at the employment centre so I can get welfare. There is no point in looking for work anymore because I do not have any transportation and my wife drinks too much to work or to help. I guess it's best if I just stay home and look after all of them."

    a. Does this client need to change? What do you think he needs to change?

    b. What does the client think he needs to do?

    c. Is this client motivated to change?

    d. How would you go about motivating this client to change?

    e. How might he react if you said he needs training during the very first interview with him?

9

Action Planning and Commitment

Chapter Goal—To help clients progress toward their goals and achieve balance by planning each step of the way ensuring they select the best options, having regard to each quadrant of the Medicine Wheel (**head**: appropriate education, **heart**: the plan is satisfying, **hands**: the skills learned are useful, **home**: values and beliefs are not compromised by the action plan).

Background—Important issues about this topic follow.
Important issues are faced by clients who own their problems and are responsible for making action plans that list each step to implement change. They will only be committed to action plans if they own them. An employment counselor's role is to provide clients with appropriate options for choosing action steps, and to ensure each action step is relevant, important and leads clients in a direct path to their desired goals.

Motivation—Why do you need to understand this?

An employment counselor must understand the boundaries of his/her responsibilities with regard to the employment issues facing clients in each of the four quadrants of the medicine wheel:

- **HEAD**—clients must acquire enough education on which to base occupational training;

- **HEART**—clients must own the problem and be motivated to do something about it;

- **HANDS**—clients must acquire appropriate skills to perform the job; and

- **HOME**—clients' values, beliefs and other life experiences must support them in their quest for a career and should not be barriers.

The job of the employment counselor is to lead clients on their quests to become self-sufficient in employment-related areas and to summon appropriate partners when they are needed to help clients achieve their goals.

Presentation—How does it work?

An action plan must be made after exploring each of the four employability dimensions. After needs or barriers are identified (see Chapter Four) under head, heart, hands and home while exploring the Job Maintenance Employability Dimension, the counselor now thinks laterally with the client and identifies options to resolve these needs or overcome these barriers. The client will select the most appropriate options and create an action plan to be implemented with the help of the employment counselor. If one of the options is to upgrade to a grade 10 level, then the action steps would be to enroll in an appropriate course, to attend that course and to pass the exams, receive grade 10 certification and finally, to return to the employment counselor to proceed to the next employability dimension where career decision making will be undertaken.

Upon the return of the client with the certificate, the employment counselor will help the client through the Career Decision Making employability dimension, again systematically checking out employment issues under each quadrant of the Medicine Wheel and creating an action plan to overcome each employment barrier or satisfy each employment need.

The same approach is used to review employment issues under Skill Enhancement and Job Search. (Each employability dimension is systematically explored using the four quadrants of the Medicine Wheel: head, heart hands and home. Action plans are created to deal with each employment issue as it arises).

It is best to proceed one employability dimension at a time because action plans may take months to complete and needs have a way of changing in the meantime. Therefore, it is best to start with the job maintenance dimension and deal with needs and barriers in that dimension, creating and implementing action plans until there are no needs left unsatisfied before proceeding to the career decision making dimension.

Clients should be made aware of their obligations during any interventions arranged on their behalf by the organization. These are as follows:

- Attending sessions, training, related programs or project activities each day, being on time and staying until they are finished;

- Making a good effort to complete all work and assignments on time;

- Advising counselors, trainers, sponsors or employers of unavoidable absences (illness, or family emergency) before start time each day;

- Arranging personal schedules (business, medical, appointments, etc.) so they are not during the session, intervention, training or project activity times;

- Spending time in home study/activities to ensure success;

- Bringing concerns to the case manager and to the counselors, trainers, sponsors, or employers who are in charge if experiencing difficulties;

- Actively participating in all activities, including job search;

- Notifying the case manager of finding work to bring the action plan up to date;

- Ensuring the case manager has a current phone number and address in order to contact a person in charge to monitor the client's progress;

- Understanding that a tax receipt (T4A) will be issued for the total amount of funding received from the program or project sponsor for the tax year;

- Understanding that the funding organization and its partners may require about six weeks to process a completed application for funding, therefore, information about whether it has been accepted will likely not be available until the end of this timeframe;

- Understanding that regular reports will be sent to the case manager about attendance and general progress and that if it is not satisfactory, the case manager will contact the client to discuss how to overcome these difficulties;

- Understanding that non-compliance with the mutually agreed-upon action plan may affect funding; and

- Notifying the case manager of any changes in circumstances within 48 hours.

Some details that must be recorded in the action plan include:

- Client's name and social insurance number (SIN);
- Name of case manager and telephone number;
- Employability dimension involved and needs or barriers under this dimension;
- How need/barrier was identified (assessment or counseling);
- Name of the service or program intervention to be applied;
- Location;
- Cost;
- Start and end date of intervention;
- Record of how intervention will address client's needs;
- Record of the mutual understanding of what "success" will be for this intervention;
- Record of how the case manager will participate in this intervention through monitoring, measuring success, getting client feedback on the quality of the intervention;
- Record of the client referral to intervention;
- Record of the advice given to the client as to the date of the next appointment after the intervention is completed;
- Showing the outcome of each intervention and whether it is considered successful; and
- If follow-up required to ascertain if clients are now employed, a record of the follow-up done and the results of the follow-up.

Once tentative action plans have been prepared by clients with the counselor's help, they should be reviewed with clients in order to ensure they fully understand and agree with what will be required of them.

After the action plan is recorded on the computer tracking system, two copies are printed and signed by both the client and the case manager/employment counselor. One copy is then given to the client and one put onto the hard copy client file. The case manager/employment counselor must be flexible and encourage the client to be flexible also, so that the action plan can be amended to address changed circumstances as needed.

After a client has made an action plan, the employment counselor is responsible for ensuring the client is carrying out each step and that each step continues to be appropriate in light of progress achieved and any changes experienced by the client. It is also critical to ensure the client remains committed to the action plan despite changes that may have occurred. This is especially important given most people's attitude to change (that change results in a loss). The employment counselor will help the client cope with changes facing him/her by looking for advantages that such a change may bring (gaining instead of losing) and by recruiting partners who will help the client cope with the change as required.

The client's first task in an action plan is to access labor market information that will cover the demand for certain occupations in the local labor market and to make an inventory of the client's interests and preferences in employment. The employment counselor would then create a decision grid (See Chapter 12) with the client listing the most important criteria to be met in order for a job to be desirable to the client. The client would be given that decision grid and given access to the profiles of jobs that are not only in demand but meet the criteria set forth by the client.

Other ways to help the client make a decision would be to chose two or three of the most appealing occupations and job shadow them, or visit a college where opportunity is provided to speak to students and instructors, or meet with willing employers to discuss working conditions. The options selected by the client become the action plan steps.

After a career has been chosen, the next step would be to select appropriate educational partners where upgrading could be undertaken if required. Upgrading becomes the next action plan step and this could last months, a year, or more. Normally, the employment counselor would monitor the client's progress through this step but if the period of attendance is over a year, the client would be asked to report back on completion of the upgrading. When upgrading is compete, career decision making MUST be reviewed again to ascertain if the client is still satisfied with his earlier career choice. If not, career decision making must be undertaken again to assess the client's new interests and desires.

Action plans for skill enhancement/occupational training, would only commence after a career decision was made and the client explored training options in terms of availability, quality, and economy. When the employment counselor agrees that the best choice has been made, application for funding authorization would be the next action step.

After funding is authorized the client's next action step is to attend training, fulfilling the obligations expected of him/her. The employment counselor is responsible for monitoring the client's progress and ensuring training costs are properly paid.

Upon successful completion of the course, the client will devise an action plan that outlines how he/she will look for work using the best approaches appropriate to the occupation for which he/she has been trained. The employment counselor would monitor the progress made by the client and use targeted wage subsidy (employer incentive), if warranted to ensure the client finds work within 90 days after the course ends so that a "found work" credit is realized by the funding organization.

Examples—Show me!

1. The client is a 38-year-old man who had an accident and can no longer do any laboring work. He has a grade eight education. He likes laboring work and is quite upset that he can no longer do this work.

   a. The client may be able to find a career that is even more desirable than laboring.

   b. The client now has an opportunity to make the same or more money and do lighter work depending on the career choice he makes.

   c. The client is young enough so that he may be able to accumulate a pension for retirement with a new career choice.

   d. The client will have a whole support network to help him in each employability dimension and under each quadrant of the Medicine Wheel.

2. The client is a 23-year-old lone parent who has just completed a registered nursing assistant course in the city. Her two children had been liv-

ing on reserve with their grandmother but now that they are both going to be in school in September (in a few months), they are coming to live with their mother in the city. She has not been able to find work and does not have childcare arranged in the city.

a.   The client is properly in the job search employability dimension but she has two issues to address: i) childcare, ii) finding a job.

b.   The employment counselor talks to her about what she perceives are her children's needs for childcare and an arrangement is made for a childcare subsidy for before and after school care. An action plan is made by the client to show how she will look for an appropriate day care and advise the employment counselor when one is found.

c.   The client's efforts to find work over the last six weeks are reviewed and the client advises she thinks she has not been hired because she has no experience and because she is a First Nations person. Targeted wage subsidy ranging from 20 to 50 per cent contribution is offered to the client as an option. Appropriate documents are prepared for the client to take with her on her job search where the subsidy is offered to an employer for a period of six months during what would be her probationary period. An action plan is created to show how the client will seek work, record the results of each contact and evaluate why she is not successful if that is the case. The action plan will also record that when an employer is found who will hire the client using the subsidy, the client will advise the employment counselor to meet with the employer to negotiate/sign the targeted wage subsidy contract.

Summary and Key Points—What is most important about this issue?

An action plan is a record of all the steps to be taken, (including all steps that need to be amended as the action plan progresses) by the client and by the employment counselor, as well as broad responsibility steps to be carried out by partners (i.e. upgrading from grades 8—11, from September to June of a given year). This action plan will cover all important aspects of activity needed to reach the employment goal of the client. The action plan will also include specific initiatives to motivate the client in dealing with changes that occur during the action plan.

Self-Test Questions—How well do I understand this?

1. A client comes to the employment counselor and advises he does not like the training he is receiving and will not want to work in the occupation for which he is being trained. The employment counselor finds out that the client is the nephew of the project sponsor who needed at least 10 participants to be part of his project. Write out an action plan you would devise with the client to rectify the situation.

2. A client comes to see the employment counselor advising he has been fired for drinking on the job. He says he has not been able to hold down any work for the last few years due to his drinking problem. Write out an action plan you would create with the client to deal with this issue under the job maintenance dimension using the Medicine Wheel to ensure all aspects of the problems are going to be addressed.

10

Communication and Feedback

Chapter Goal—To achieve a balanced style of communication.

Background—Important issues about this topic follow.
An important issue in communication is to understand that communication is an <u>exchange</u> between two or more people or other live beings. It is not always oral (talking, barking, meowing, etc.). Often it is a display of behaviors such as shaking a finger to warn someone, winking, a dog biting someone, or a cat switching its tail back and forth. In addition, communication sometimes requires that those involved in it stop talking, barking, meowing, etc. long enough to listen and watch in order to get the messages that are being sent in ways other than orally (a growling dog is probably telling you he might bite you ...). It has been said of meditation that people need to stop talking to God (praying) long enough to listen (meditate) in order to hear God's answer to their prayers.

Motivation—Why do you need to understand this?

Employment counselors need to achieve and maintain balance in all four quadrants of the Medicine Wheel in order to properly communicate with clients to identify needs, make action plans, and encourage them to achieve success.

Presentation—How does it work?

<u>Influences of Communication</u>

1. Communication is not only accomplished through words and actions, but it is also done with space, tone and volume.

People feel uncomfortable when others get too close to them. This is called the "space factor." Did you know that 36 inches around a person constitutes "public space?" Thirty to 36 inches around a person is considered "social space." Trustworthy people who are well known can move closer, within 24 inches of the person, into the "personal space." Family or other intimately known persons can move in closer than 24 inches, into the "intimate space." Violating another's space can damage relationship building.

Meaning also comes from *how* something is said. The tone and volume of certain words in a sentence can change its meaning. Read this sentence to yourself and emphasize the bold word in each reading, taking note of the different meanings that emerge.

I did not say she stole the ring.
I **did** not say she stole the ring.
I did **not** say she stole the ring.
I did not **say** she stole the ring.
I did not say **she** stole the ring.
I did not say she **stole** the ring.
I did not say she stole **the** ring.
I did not say she stole the **ring.**

2. Communication is also influenced by gender, race, age, region, culture, occupations and hobbies. The overall impact of such influences is to *exclude* those who are not insiders or a part of the group using the language. A good example of this kind of *lingo* is the kind being used today in text messaging. The workplace usually has its own language that is developed on the basis of the technical requirements of the job as well as whether the workplace is populated predominantly by women or men, and if they are older or younger, and so forth. Employment counselors are expected to speak without using such lingo that may be unfamiliar to clients and make them **uncomfortable.**

3. The Medicine Wheel has a big impact on how one communicates. If a quadrant is out of balance, the person will be deemed to have a definite style of speaking and it may not be pleasant. Below are a few examples of how the Medicine Wheel may show the impacts of speech:

HEAD—where a person is highly educated and uses vocabulary that is beyond the comprehension of those to whom he/she is speaking;

HEART—where a person is very emotional and uses "flowery" language that people find uncomfortable in every day speech;

HANDS—where a person uses work or technical lingo to speak to others outside work or outside the group who normally use the lingo; where one uses body language, consciously or unconsciously to send messages (using hand or head gestures); and

HOME—where a person uses a dialect that is known only to people from his/her home area.

One way to improve speaking skills is to join an organization such as Toastmaster's or other clubs where people gather to practice their speaking skills.

Counselor Communication Styles

1. Types of Questioning

Using an open style of questioning with clients will yield better results than a closed style. Open style means you avoid questions that can be answered by a simple "yes" or "no." Instead, use words like, "what, how and why" to get clients talking and to put them at ease. In your interviews, it is important for clients to talk and for the employment counselor to listen!

Some Common mistakes in questioning are:

- Changing the question midway
- Asking two questions at once
- Answering one's own question
- Using the question at the expense of the client (did you leave your last job because you didn't like it?)
- Bombarding client with too many questions
- Overusing closed questions
- Ambiguous questions

2. Sympathy & Empathy

Sympathy is normally extended during times of loss and means someone feels sorry/sad for the problems being faced by another person. It may include an effort to comfort the other person. Empathy is deeper than sympathy. It means that you are also "walking in the client's moccasins" or have walked in them before and know from first hand experience what the client faces. Some people, even though they have not had the same experience, have had very similar ones that make them empathetic also.

3. Respectfulness

Each culture has its own notions of how to express respect. In some parts of the world, burping is a sign of appreciation and respect after eating a meal. In many native cultures averting one's eyes before someone of importance is considered polite. You can probably think of six different behaviors that illustrate your notion of respectfulness.

4. Concreteness

Interviewers who identify the specific feelings, attitudes, beliefs, experiences, and behaviors impacting on the client are being concrete. Concreteness is the fluent, direct, and complete expression of specific feelings and experiences regardless of their emotional content. This serves three purposes in an interview:

a. It keeps the counselor's response close to the client's feelings and experiences.

b. It fosters accurate understanding while letting the client correct misunderstandings.

c. It lets the client focus on specific problem areas.

Overall, concreteness helps to focus on issues. Clients can be helped to become more concrete in interviewers by:

- being role models who are specific in their own communication;

- asking for examples using "how" and "what" regarding feelings, attitudes, etc.;

- helping clients to be more specific about their feelings; and

- encouraging, clarifying, elaborating and specifying.

5. Genuineness

This is when the interviewer practices what he/she preaches, where he/she "walks the talk." This will be apparent to clients. The attributes of the interviewer are apparent in the actual reality of the interviewer's life. Clients can believe in the honesty and sincerity of the interviewer; genuineness can reassure by giving order and unity to clients.

When clients experience authenticity with an interviewer, there is a good opportunity for personal growth whereby clients move toward good psychological health as in Maslow's Hierarchy of Needs.

Listening Is Key To Good Communication

1. Attentive Listening

The ability to <u>listen</u> to what another is saying is the most important part of communication. With this skill, one can gain much knowledge, learn new things and become adept at problem solving as well as resolving conflict. Making friends and establishing good relationships is easier when one listens closely to what others say. People who feel you are listening to and understanding them will cooperate with you and return the respect you show to them.

A good listener may help to reduce tension by giving another person the chance to "let off steam." Effective listening also staves off conflict in that one can take the time to decide a wiser course of action rather than "putting one's foot in his or her mouth." Taking the time to listen provides a window of opportunity, to do a better job by absorbing ideas for improvement. It also helps to increase one's enjoyment of life i.e. movies; television; lectures; plays; music; and good conversation. Being a good listener is a gift to one's family and friends—it will help to solidify these relationships and allow one to "walk in the other's moccasins."

2. Reflective Listening

This is a technique to facilitate communication with clients. Reflective listening seeks understanding, not necessarily agreement. It is an attentive, respectful, non-judgmental approach to interviewing for identification of employment needs and counseling. There are three basic levels of reflective listening:

a.   Repeating or rephrasing with repetition (word content)

b.   Paraphrasing using your own words without repeating (word and meaning content)

c.   Reflection of feeling (share your perception of the client's meaning and feelings in own words)

Reflective listening is particularly helpful in breaking down barriers and minimizing resistance with persons who are angry or frustrated. It does not try to control but to empower people. Success will only be achieved when the interviewer really cares about the person being interviewed.

The Five "Don'ts" of Reflective Listening

- Don't parrot.

- Don't listen without empathy.

- Don't open the door then slam it shut (by jumping to conclusions, to solutions, to evaluation or to punishment).

- Don't use bad timing (by using reflection when all that is being asked is for information).

- Don't analyze (adding your guess why the speaker feels the way they do, instead ask them why when you have a chance if you really don't yet know why).

3. Summarizing to promote effective communication.

Summaries show your client how effectively you have been listening by clearly reflecting what has been said. This is part of reflective listening and promotes good communication. Summaries should be used periodically during the interview to ensure you as the interviewer, are still on track and to check your understanding of what the client has been telling you. They are especially helpful at transition points, as at the end of the interview, before going on to the action plan. Therefore, it is wise to take notes during the interview so that you have highlights that may be included in the summary. Be sure to tell the client what you are doing so they do not become uncomfortable with the recording of their dialogue.

Summaries may begin with the following statements:

a.   Let me see if I understand so far …

b.   Here is what I have heard. Tell me if I have missed anything.

Summaries should give special attention to "change" statements. Such statements might be paraphrased or reflected with the client's feeling back to the client. Change statements might look like this:

1.   Problem recognition: I need more education.

2.   Concern: If I do not get my grade 12, I will never find a job.

3.   Intent to change: If I do not hurry up and get my grade 12, I'll be old and gray.

4.   Optimism: I know I can get my grade 12; I just have to buckle down.

The summary should always include these statements back to the client as these open the door to taking positive action for change. If the person still seems undecided after the interview, this observation should be included in the summary showing both sides of what the client is considering. It could be done by stating: "On one hand, (use his/her name) says/feels … yet on the other hand he/she says/feels …" This helps to clarify the choices that must be made for the client. If there are documents that relate to the client's employment issues (medicals, certificates, etc.) it is good to include these in the summary. Be concise. End with an invitation to the client to add what you might have missed, to clarify certain points, and to correct points if necessary. The summary itself may help the client to make appropriate decisions for the action plan.

4. Feedback—A Critical Part of Communication

In helping clients achieve their action plans, employment counselors will be required to give <u>feedback</u>. The way feedback is provided will often spell the success of clients in achieving their employment goals. Therefore, it is important for employment counselors to know how to provide feedback that is honest, meaningful, and challenging without crushing spirits.

Feedback may be corrective. When such feedback is given, one must remember to be hard on the problem and easy on the person. Feedback must always identify the problem and help to provide a solution. If a solution has not been provided, the client and the interviewer should work together to find a mutually agreed-upon solution to be implemented.

Feedback should normally be:

a.   Requested

b.   Motivated by a desire to help

c.   Non-judgmental

d.   Timely

e.   Specific and direct

Good employment counseling will utilize feedback as a key communication tool in guiding clients' progress through the action plan. "Sandwiching" the feedback—giving positive feedback at the outset, negative feedback at the mid-point and more positive feedback at the end—makes the negative feedback easier to "swallow."

Another way to deliver negative feedback is to find something clients are doing right and challenge them to do it in other specific areas. This is called the "strength-challenge" and it encourages clients to improve their performance.

The following guidelines will help counselors to provide valuable feedback to their clients:

a.   Be sure clients are ready to receive feedback otherwise it will be misinterpreted.

b.   Use "I" statements (start your feedback with the word "I").

c.   Be respectful and authentic so clients do not go away feeling they are not as good as you. Try to lace in some of your own personal feelings and concerns when giving feedback.

d.   Give feedback immediately in relation to a recent event so clients will remember it.

e.   Describe the behavior without being judgmental.

f.   Be specific, using quotes and examples whenever possible.

g.   Ensure clients understand the feedback and its intention.

h.   Target behaviors that can be changed.

i.   Ensure your intention is to help clients.

j.   Focus on one or two key areas at a time for feedback so as not to over-whelm clients.

5. Receiving Feedback Gracefully

This is as important as giving feedback. It is only through feedback that you learn about how you are performing: good, fair or poor. This affords the opportunity for improvement. Feedback is an arrow pointing directly to success! However, you want feedback that tells you about what you want to know. Therefore, here are some rules for receiving feedback:

a.   When inviting feedback, state what you want feedback about so that it is focused.

b.   Check what you have heard to ensure you understand the feedback.

c.   Share your reactions to the feedback advising what you found helpful. The receiver should help encourage the person to give good feedback because this is truly how one can improve. The person giving the feedback must feel it is appreciated in order to continue providing feedback.

The most important thing to remember about receiving feedback is that it is usually only given by people who care enough to "stick their neck" out to do so. Therefore, people receiving it should accept it sincerely and deal with it honestly.

6. Poor Listening Habits

The inability to listen adequately creates barriers to effective communication. The following are some habits of the ineffective listener:

a.   **On-Off Listening**—Most people think about four times as fast as the average person speaks, leaving a listener with three quarters of a minute extra thinking time to reflect on personal issues or other areas of concern. *(Suggested solution: Use the extra time to pay attention to more than the words, watching non-verbal signs like gestures, eye contact, hesitation and voice tone to capture the essence of what is being said.)*

b.   **Red Flag Listening**—Some words, ideas, or opinions will trigger a negative reaction in us and we may stop listening. These expressions are often cultural, political, or religious and make us react like a bull in front of a red flag. *(Suggested solution: Discover our own personal red flags and keep them in check.)*

c. **Open Ears—Closed Mind Listening**—We may decide at the start that either the subject or the speaker is boring and what is being said makes no sense. We decide we can predict what the person will say and there is no point in listening because we will hear nothing new. *(Suggested solution: Better to listen and be sure there is nothing new than to make assumptions.)*

d. **Glassy-Eyed Listening**—We may look at a person intently and seem to be listening but our minds are absorbed in our own thoughts. We become glassy-eyed with a dreamy expression. We can tell when other people are glassy-eyed and they can also see it in us. *(Suggested solution: Postpone daydreaming and if tired, suggest a break or change of pace.)*

e. **Too-Complicated-For-Me Listening**—When we find ideas too detailed or complex, we stop paying attention and give up trying to understand. *(Suggested solution: It is important to keep asking clarifying questions to understand.)*

f. **Don't-Rock-The-Boat Listening**—We don't like to have our ideas, prejudices and points of view challenged or overturned. So when someone says something with which we do not agree we may stop listening or even become defensive and then counter-attack. *(Suggested solution: You should keep listening carefully and non-defensively so you can do a better job of responding constructively.)*

7. Some Styles of Poor Listening

Ineffective, or poor listening skills create important challenges to communication, as the following demonstrates:

a. **The Faker**—This type of listener pretends to listen. Their demeanor suggests they are listening intently (they smile and nod their heads) but in reality, they are thinking about something else. Wanting to appear as though they are listening, they concentrate on "striking a pose," thereby using up their "listening energy."

b. **The Dependent Listener**—This style of listener's main concern is that the speaker has a good impression of them. Therefore, they agree with whatever the speaker says because they want to maintain goodwill at all costs.

c. **The Interrupter Listener**—They never let the speaker finish what he/she has to say. This listener may be afraid that they will forget what they want to say or feel they must respond to a point as soon as it is made. They may also be more concerned with their own thoughts and feelings rather than those of others. They barrage the speaker with questions instead of listening.

d. **The Self-Conscious Listener**—They are more concerned about their own status in the eyes of the speaker/other persons rather than the ideas and feelings of others. They try to impress and don't listen with understanding.

e. **The Intellectual Listener**—This style of listener focuses on the words of the speaker to make an appraisal of the message being delivered. They ignore non-verbal cues i.e. body language as they are too focused on being logical and systematic. They may have developed a manner of listening in their occupations, which did not require other styles of listening.

f. **The Judge and Jury Listener**—This style of listener is so busy judging the ideas or behavior of others that they do not listen. They may say the other person/speaker is wrong and attack them without trying to understand their position. They become deaf to any ideas but their own.

8. The Golden Rules of Effective Listening, as listed below, will help break barriers to good communication:

a. Stop talking.

b. Put the speaker at ease.

c. Pay attention to non-verbal language.

d. Listen for what is not said.

e. Know exactly what the other person is saying.

f. Be aware of "tune out" words.

g. Concentrate on "hidden" emotional meanings.

h. Be patient.

i.   Hold your temper.

j.   Empathize with the speaker.

Examples—Show me!

1.   "Get out of my space!" says a woman to an aggressive man on a bus. (personal space)

2.   "Spam" and "blogs" are internet lingo.

3.   "Yes, OK, I'll do it …" but the person is shaking their head saying "no." (body language)

4.   A student keeps talking during class so that he is not listening to the instructor. (this poor listening shows disrespect)

5.   The client says: "I don't want to be an apprentice because the work is too hard." You, as the counselor say: "You feel apprenticing is too labor intensive?" This reflective listening invites the client to clarify what he told you.

6.   "Let me see if I have this right, you want to get your grade 10 and then go into pre-apprenticeships training to be a carpenter?" (summarizing)

7.   "I am concerned about all of the time you have missed from your classes. How do you intend to catch up?" (feedback using an "I" statement and an open question)

8.   "I require feedback on the way I have been doing follow-up with you. Is it better done by telephone or in writing by letter?" (feedback using an "I" statement and a closed question)

Summary and Key Points—What is most important about this issue?

Communication will make or break a relationship. If you are poor at communicating with others, employment counseling will be difficult for you and the results you achieve will not be good. Therefore, it is important to pay attention to how you communicate and make conscious efforts to improve your ability in this area. Above all, be a good listener as this trait will make up for shortfalls in oral speech.

Using the Medicine Wheel to achieve a balanced approach to communicating.

HEAD—Most people are comfortable with a grade eight or nine vocabulary level, so save the big words for another day. Keep your thoughts on what the client is saying, ensuring you are not daydreaming.

HEART—Be sincere in all you say and do. Honesty will always be reflected in how you say what you are saying ... or it will not. Once you lose a client's trust, you may never get it back. Do not let emotions cloud your perceptions. This is why you should not be dealing with your relatives or close friends, in order to maintain an objective and fair approach.

HANDS—Be congruent, ensuring your body language is sending the same message as your words. Don't fiddle with things while you are listening, as this gives the client the impression that you are bored, or impatient.

HOME—Use grammatical English to say what needs to be said. Avoid dialect if possible unless your client only understands dialect. Use an interpreter (First Nations Languages, or French, for example) to speak with people if necessary. You cannot communicate well with someone if they have trouble understanding you. Don't let the fact that the client has a different value/belief system from you interfere with your ability to listen. Avoid condemnation because you do not agree with something he/she has said. Try to see it from the other's point of view and if you still disagree, then you must decide if this issue constitutes a barrier or a need that you will be required to deal with.

Self-Test Questions—How well do I understand this?

1. Give an example of a statement that would be insulting to a person of another race.

2. Give an example of body language. What quadrant of the Medicine Wheel is at play when body language is used?

3. Why is your experience that is similar to your client's empathic?

4. What is reflective listening?

5. What communication technique can close off one part of an interview and lead into the next?

6. Why is feedback important to both you and your client?

11

Negotiation

Chapter Goal—To achieve balance in communication that leads to "win-win" goals instead of "win-lose" goals.

Background—Important issues about this topic follow.
Important issues in this chapter are to understand that "negotiation" might very well be another word for "employment counseling" since successful negotiation relies on satisfying the needs of both negotiating parties: the employment counselor and the client. This is done by exploring possible options and finding a solution that represents a "win" for each of the parties.

Motivation—Why do you need to understand this?

Good employment counseling is based on establishing a healthy relationship with the other party (client). Both must agree on a "win–win solution" (WWS). For the client, the WWS is the realization of his/her employment goal. The employment counselor shares in the WWS when the client's employment goal is achieved, thereby fulfilling the vision and mission of the organization.

Presentation—How does it work?

A paramount principle to remember in all your negotiations is to seek out and agree upon a WWS rather than one where one party wins and the other loses. The loss for one party leaves bitter feelings and reduces the stature of the winning party. Most people, including employment counselors, want people with whom they have dealings to remember them for their fairness and caring attitudes, not for any perceived greed and desire to win at any cost.

There are certain approaches that will help you to negotiate the best deal for yourself AND for the other party. Briefly, here are some things you can do using the Medicine Wheel to map out options:

HEAD—Ensure you know what you and your party (your organization, family, or client) want the "win" to look like. In this regard, you should also know what the other party wants as well as what the other party *thinks* you want. This may be important because the other party may be willing to give you more than you expect to gain.

You should also know your Best Alternative To a Negotiated Agreement (BATNA) as well as the other party's BATNA. The BATNA represents the second best result in a negotiation and is quite often what one of the parties will have to accept in place of a WWS.

HEART—When preparing for the negotiation clearly assess your feelings, ensuring you do not hurry or are not so desperate to win the other party over to your way of thinking as this will surely harm the trust and the relationship you are working to establish. Any future interaction with the other party will be difficult and make negotiation almost impossible. It would be better for another person to take over the role of negotiator if the relationship is ruined. Visualize a line where you stand on one end and the other party at the other end. Most people's inclination is to play tug of war where one side gives in to the other. However, if you look around you, in ever expanding circles from where you and your negotiating partner have taken positions, you might find the solution that pleases both of you in that ever-widening circle of possibilities!

HANDS—Consciously set out to build trust with the other party. This means you will try to be relaxed, friendly and approachable. Being a good listener will also help to make the other party comfortable. If you enjoy the process, other parties will too; if you don't, neither will they. Above all, be honest and do not try to hide anything. It is best to admit the truth even if it is damaging to your side. Listen with your eyes and ears to get the real message the other side is conveying to you. Their mouths may be saying one thing but their body language might be saying something else.

Be sure the room you have chosen for the negotiation is comfortable and worthy of the person with whom you will negotiate. Meeting in a back alley for such a talk is not suitable for a legitimate, respectable discussion. In addition, if a room is too noisy, too hot, too cold, too dusty, too crowded, etc., your chances for success are diminished.

HOME—Learn as much as you can about the other party so you are ready to engage them in meaningful discussion about issues they value. As well, you should know their style of negotiation. Do they believe in winning at all costs and therefore would use threats and aggression to make certain the other party loses? They may be unprincipled, without conscience and care little for the other party. Some negotiators have hidden agendas and regard winning a "win-lose" type of negotiation as a bonus because not only do they get what they want but they leave the other side "hurt and bleeding" so they will not be able to pose any threat in the future.

When you have been invited to a negotiating table, you have as much power as the other party with whom you are negotiating. Both parties like to give the impression that they have all the power in a negotiation, but if that was true, they would have no need to negotiate with you. It is best to believe you are as powerful as the other party and given your desire to reach a win-win you should pose no threat to the other party. Therefore, who is most powerful is not important unless the other party intends to use their power to do damage. In that case, there are methods of turning the destructive power back onto those who would use it. (You may read about such approaches in one of the many available books on negotiating.)

The negotiating process breaks into three distinct phases and compares with the interview process that we will examine in the next chapter. The three phases are:

1. **Before the negotiation**—prepare by ensuring all those things that can be done before sitting down to negotiate have been done.

2. **During the negotiation**—set the tone to establish comfort and trust and to explore options to find one that can be agreed upon. Review the record of the negotiation to ensure nothing was missed or misinterpreted.

3.   **After the negotiation**—review how it progressed, noting what went well and what needed improvement. Use this information in future negotiations.

Examples—Show me!

1.   You are the negotiator for five staff members who are about to be fired because your employer says he can save money by contracting out your jobs. On discussing the employer's offer to contract you find that there will be a fair hike in wages being offered to the contractors although benefits will not be paid. After consulting with your party members, you find that the increase in money to be paid to contractors would cover the costs of private medical insurance as well as the purchase of a registered retirement savings certificate each year. In fact, when the new self-employed status being offered is fully considered, you would be paying less taxes with the result that you would actually have more take home pay. You find that the employer's offer to contract the staff instead of employ them is a win for you and your party as well as for the employer.

2.   The other party in the negotiation says they have reserved a location for the meeting and have provided you with an address to attend. When you try to locate the meeting place you find out you have been given the wrong address. A phone call to the other party results in you waiting for 15 minutes for someone to talk to you. When you finally speak to someone from the other party he is annoyed that you are going to be late and after giving you the correct address, hangs up the phone. Swallowing your anger you drive to the meeting place and find the correct room. You are wearing a tailored suit in honor of the occasion but everyone else in the room is wearing t-shirts and shorts. You are the only woman in the room and all the others (five of them) are men ranging from 24 to 62 years old. They are seated with their backs to a bank of windows and there is a fan blowing air directly at them from the side of the room. On the table in front of their chairs stands a pitcher of water with glasses ready if they need them. There is no water or glass in front of your chair. They do not pause in their discussion of the football game when you enter. Finally you are asked to sit down on the other side of the table with full sunlight bearing down upon you.

You realize that the other party's plan is to upset, intimidate, and make you so angry you will not be able to negotiate properly. The problem is that you really are upset and angry and in no condition to negotiate. You know that time is a big factor for you and also for them and that a good agreement is necessary as soon as possible. But, you do not want to be pushed into a situation that is uncomfortable for you. You stand up, gather your things, retrieve your business cards and hand them out to each man on the other side of the table. Then you tell them that you will be in touch tomorrow after you arrange a better milieu for the negotiation and you leave. You have sent them a message that you will not tolerate "dirty tricks" and the next day, you show them to a comfortable air-conditioned room where coffee and snacks are waiting in welcome. There is no need to "get even" because this is not a contest. Being fair-minded and up-front will be more conducive to achieving WWS for both parties.

Summary and Key Points—What is most important about this issue?

Negotiation is about finding a mutually acceptable solution to a problem by forming a trusting relationship with another party facing the same dilemma. The main idea in negotiation is to take the time to find a solution where both you and the other party can pull in the *same direction* to get to the "win." Everything possible must be done to get both parties facing the problem from the same point of view. This *always* means that the two parties are not facing each other from opposite sides and playing "tug of war" but exploring options that are not part of the straight line between you and the other party.

Self-Test Questions—How well do I understand this?

1. Your proposal for a solution is considered by the two people negotiating for the other party. They say that if it was up to them, they would agree on the suggested solution but they know that their boss would not accept the proposal. What would you do next?

2. The union representative says they need a 20% raise in wages; travel allowance of $5/kilometer; unlimited training allowances; $200/daily living allowances; and $50/daily incidentals. Since the job requires travel 80% of the time, the final wages for one employee, given all these demands, would work out to $935,000 (approximately) per year. The drivers had been previously earning $120,000 per year. The cost of living increase was 5%. What would you do as the negotiator for the employer?

12

Decision Grids—Using Transparency in Decision Making

Chapter Goal—To achieve balance in rendering decisions that are consistently fair and objective.

Background—Important issues about this topic follow.
Important issues surface when decision makers are accused of playing favorites. They may not consider similar sets of factors or *consistently* weigh such factors in making their decisions. When decisions are subject to appeal, it is critical to have a "standard yardstick" for making decisions. "Eligibility criteria" for funding clients is an example of how to make decisions more transparent, fair and accountable.

Motivation—Why do you need to understand this? Although employment counselors may use this method of making decisions in their personal lives, this approach is particularly suited to helping clients make career decisions. Clients may base decisions on factors they find personally desirable. Therefore, clients create their own decision-making criteria.

Presentation—How does it work?
A decision grid is a tool to help make objective decisions based on a set of criteria that the decision maker establishes. When used as a hiring tool, it ensures all candidates are measured using the same yardstick (criteria). Eligibility criteria for funding are also a form of decision grid. Such criteria help to screen out unsuitable candidates/options and rate the suitable candidates against established rating criteria.

A decision grid may be used with clients to help them make career decisions based on factors that are important to them. This is the same for clients who want to go into training. They must also satisfy certain criteria to be eligible for funding and be rated against a list of rating criteria so that the best qualified candidates may be selected.

Normally there are two sets of criteria established for a decision grid: **screening** criteria and **rating** criteria. There can be two or three <u>screening</u> criteria (preferably no more than three) that serve to screen out unsuitable options at the start. The client/option either meets this screening criteria or does not.

There may be up to 10 (usually no more) <u>rating</u> criteria where points are assigned as follows:

Very good: **2** points, Satisfactory: **1** point; Unsatisfactory: **0** Points

Assigning more than two points in a rating scale means you are forced into defining how four points is better than three, and how five points is better than four. You will also need to show clearly the differences between three and four, etc. to justify your marks. This becomes complicated and allows too much leeway for personal judgment.

Examples—Show me!

See next page for chart on how a decision grid was used and the page after for a blank sample of a decision grid.

Below is an example of a decision grid on buying a car.

Screening Criteria	If no, car is screened out
i. Must be 5 years old or less	☐ Yes (rated) ☐ No
ii. Must cost $5000 or less	☐ Yes ☐ No
Rating Criteria	**Points: 2-very good, 1-satisfactory, 0-unsatisfactory**
1. Has less than 160,000 km	**Points awarded:**
2. Has good tires	**Points awarded:**
3. Has power steering	**Points awarded:**
4. Has auto transmission	**Points awarded:**
5. Car is clean	**Points awarded:**
6. Has no rust	**Points awarded:**
7. Has air conditioning	**Points awarded:**
8. Has power windows, locks	**Points awarded:**
	Total Points:

When shopping for a vehicle you would assess each car you consider against this grid and select the one with the most points.

Summary and Key Points - What is most important about this issue?

Decision grids guarantee fairness, consistency, and transparency in decision-making. It is important that such criteria be freely shared with those who supply the product being evaluated by the decision grid.

Those applying for jobs must know the qualifying (screening) criteria or requirements and the rating criteria so they understand how they scored.

Decision Grid
Step 1: Screening Criteria

1.	Yes	No
2.	Yes	No

If all answers to the criteria in step 1 are "yes", then go on to step 2.	
Step 2: Rating Criteria	
Point System:3 - Excellent, 2 - Satisfactory, 1 - Poor, 0	**Points Awarded**
1.	
2.	
3.	
4.	
5.	
6.	
7.	
8.	
Total: **To achieve passing mark** **16 or more points to achieve 66%** **12 points to achieve 50%** **11 points or less fails**	

Self-Test Questions—How well do I understand this?

1. Why is it important to have clearly established decision-making criteria in the event of an appeal against a decision to deny funding?

2. Who should be making up the criteria in a decision-making grid and why (think about this in terms of the consumer of the service and the supplier of the service)?

13

The Four Phases of an Employment Counseling Interview

Chapter Goal—To use a balanced approach in client interviews for maximum effectiveness, efficiency and client comfort and satisfaction.

Background—Important issues about this topic follow.
Important issues to understand about interviewing are that clients and employment counselors feel more secure if they have an interview pattern they know works well, and that they have practiced many times so there is no hesitation in leading the client through each interview phase.

Motivation—Why do you need to understand this?

Employment counselors use the four-phase interview system as a tool along with the Medicine Wheel and the four employability dimensions to help lead clients to achieve their employment goals, in a systematic way. Once the employment counselor feels comfortable using these tools, the client will also feel comfortable and confident that the employment counselor is knowledgeable and trustworthy.

Presentation—How does it Work?

This is a client centered approach that means:

1. Early intervention is needed to address clients' employment needs.

2. Clients recognize their needs with a counselor's help.

3.   Clients participate in the entire counseling process and make their own decisions based on what they think is best for them with the help of a counselor.

4.   Counselors discharge their duty to clients by ensuring they present a variety of options to clients from which they can make their choices, having regard to the client's personal and community resources.

The chart on the next page outlines the four phases of interviews along with the components of each phase. A detailed description of each phase will then follow.

The four phases that may be used by employment counselors with clients are outlined in the chart below:

First Phase ➡ Identify the Employment Issue

a) Establish a collaborative relationship (learn to blend with client).
b) State the employment issue.
c) Formulate the constraint statement (I can't find work because...).
d) Establish the purpose of the interview (Today we will...).

Second Phase ➡ Determine Needs In the Four Employability Dimensions

e) Using the Medicine Wheel, clarify the client's education (head), emotional issues (heart) such as the job loss cycle, etc., the client's skills/training and abilities (hands) and take note of values and beliefs expressed by the client from the things she/he says during the interview (home's influence on client).
f) Clarify what personal resources the client brings in light of what is available in the community. Recognize the barriers that will need to be overcome.

Third Phase ➡ Action Planning In Each Dimension

g) Create contingency statements and establish counseling goals (each of the four employability dimensions may have a counseling goal if there are needs in that dimension).
h) Generate, validate and prioritize options (with the client, choose the best, second best, etc. steps to achieve the goal in that dimension).
i) Together with the client make the action plan to achieve goals in each employability dimension.

Fourth Phase ➡ Case Management & Results

j) Each step of the action plan must be case managed to ensure it has been completed successfully by the client. An amended action plan may be needed to address new difficulties encountered by the client.
k) Ideally, follow-up occurs after all the steps of the action plan have been completed to see if the client found work and/or if client is self-sufficient i.e. he/she has no more needs or has learned how to satisfy his/her own needs in each employability dimension and does not need any further assistance from the counselor. Otherwise, follow-up may begin soon after the client fails to report to the counselor at the time that was pre-arranged.

Following is an in-depth description of the four phases involved in a counselor/client interview.

First Phase—Identify the Employment Issue
Part a) Establishing a Collaborative Relationship

Establishing a collaborative relationship depends almost exclusively on one's ability to communicate well. As we have seen, communication is done through words, actions, space, tone, and volume. It is influenced by gender and race. As well, counselors must behave with <u>respect</u> and <u>genuineness</u> to forge a solid relationship with a client.

Important to remember is that the first contact between a counselor and a client may be laced with the client's emotions and anxiety, making the client difficult to get along with. Therefore, counselors must be sensitive to client's perceptions and feelings to try to minimize the impact of their own reactions to the client's behavior. The counselor must always be straightforward, honest, respectful and genuine.

In subsequent interviews, as the contact between the client and the counselor deepens and information is exchanged, it may become necessary to be the bearer of bad news (perhaps about funding eligibility for example). Such information must be delivered objectively and without any element of "blame." It should also be coupled with alternatives the client may consider. This is all a part of "blending" with the client. The client should feel that his/her loss is important to the counselor and that the counselor will work to help him or her make other suitable arrangements. Clients should never be forced to "sink or swim" on their own just because they are not eligible for funding by the organization.

Part b) State the Employment Issue

This is a key part of the interview because it is here that a client may provide signals about his or her perception of the employment issue. Do not attempt to clarify it at this point, but record the client's statement <u>just as it was told to you.</u> Clients will normally say why they are here and this statement may provide some insight into the client's problem.

Do not judge the client on the basis of this statement. We must respect the client's call for help and be genuine in our response to him/her. This statement is the first signpost to show the challenges facing the client including the client's opinion about changes he/she needs to make or is awaiting. We are being invited to be his/her helpers in dealing with the change or in helping out while he/she waits for the change to happen. Depending on what is discovered during later interviews, we may need the expertise of community partners to deal with employment barriers facing the client.

Following are some examples of statements made to counselors by clients about their perception of the problem. These statements tell you a lot about whether or not this client owns his/her problem:

"They took my license away so I have no way to look for work. I need bus tickets."

"Nobody will hire me as an auto mechanic so I need training in welding."

"Nobody wants to hire me! It is not as if I have not had jobs before … I've had loads of jobs!"

"My employer no longer needs any typists and I will be laid off by the end of this month. I came in to see about training for a new type of work."

"I have five kids and my husband walked out on us. I need training for a job that pays good money so I can support my kids."

"The last time I was here you guys didn't help me at all. I'm giving you one more chance to fund me for modeling or I will go to my chief!"

Part c) Formulate the Constraint Statement

After the client presents the employment problem from his/her own point of view and the counselor records it, the counselor asks the client why he/she thinks this problem exists (cause) from the client's perspective. The counselor may suggest the client complete the following statement: "I cannot find work **because** …" This will be the constraint statement as perceived by the client. It represents a "stalled" position where the client is trapped.

The first part of the constraint statement describes the client's problem and the second part tells the client's perception of the cause of the problem. Again, this should be recorded in the client's own words. It is important for the counselor to understand the client's perception of the cause of his/her employment difficulty. A client may be unclear about why he/she is experiencing the problem (I don't know why I can't find work.) or they may not recognize what their constraint is at this point. If this is the case, clients will likely need to go through all four employability dimensions to identify employment needs and/or barriers.

The reason given by the client for his/her employment difficulty or constraint, whether it is valid or not, becomes the purpose of this particular interview. (Later, after the purpose of this interview is established, the client is assisted to explore his/her needs/barriers under the different employability dimensions using the four quadrants of the medicine wheel.)

An example of a counselor repeating a constraint statement such as: "You have problems in finding work as a truck driver because you have never had to look for work before," gives the client the opportunity to agree with or to clarify the problem once again. After the issue as perceived by the client is clear to the counselor, the counselor proceeds to tell the client the purpose of the interview.

Part d) Establish the Purpose of the Interview

Agreement on the purpose of the interview is only reached after ensuring both the counselor and client clearly understand the problem and its cause, as perceived by the client. The client's perception of the problem should be clearly demonstrated by the constraint statement. It will likely establish the purpose of the current interview that is, in most cases, to go on to the needs determination phase of the interview so that each of the client's specific employment needs are identified and addressed. It should be noted that the client's perception of the problem and its cause may be **altogether different from the actual root cause of the employment difficulty.** The root cause may not surface until other steps to clarify needs have been undertaken. Often identification of root causes is gradual, like peeling the layers of an onion.

During the first interview, it is important to deal with the client's perception of the cause and discuss how you can work together with the client to help (needs determination and action planning). It is also important for the counselor to be clear on the client's expectations. The counselor is obliged to immediately advise the client if these expectations can be addressed or not. The mandate of the organization may not allow for certain needs or barriers to be addressed so that referral out to partners is required.

Questions that may be used by the counselor to lead clients into needs determination interviews include:

- How do you see us working together to deal with your problem?
- What do you want me to do to help you?
- What services can we provide to help you?

Through such questions the counselor will be able to assess the client's understanding of what the organization can do and how the counselor might be able to help. It is during this period that the counselor must also explain what service the client can expect by describing the interview process and how it may help to identify some possible solutions. The client must be asked if he/she wants to continue with this process.

While such discussion is underway, the counselor must be alert to identify any signs of resistance and to take the time to deal with any reluctance expressed by the client. If the client does not buy into the process at this point and the counselor fails to convince him/her of the value of the services being offered, the interview should end with the counselor requesting the client to think about what is being offered and provide brochures on the services available. As the client will probably leave at this point he/she should always be invited to use the self-service facilities.

Those who are committed to the process and fully understand what will be happening are ready to participate in exploring their service needs.

Highlights of First Phase Interview Process:

1. Take time to use your best communication skills to put the client at ease and to present a friendly, helpful approach. (This may involve small talk if the client is not too stressed.)

2. Record the client's statement, verbatim, about the employment issue. This statement may provide clues to you about whether the client owns the problem or if he/she is waiting for things to get better. (Internal/external locus of control)

3. Write the constraint statement with the client's help: "I can't find work because ..." and ask why this condition exists (to confirm locus of control or ideas about causes of client's difficulties). Client's replies to these

questions will help situate employment issues in appropriate employ-ability dimensions and in quadrants of the Medicine Wheel, but if there are two or more employability dimensions involved, it is probably best to plan on covering them all with the client in needs determination.

4. Establish the purpose of the interview—"Today we will review the fol-lowing areas":

- **Employment Maintenance**: Explore client's past work history to see where he/she ran into problems (or look at other problems that may be evident from the registration form or the client's own advice to you).

- **Career Decision Making**: Decide if client feels he/she is in a desir-able career and/or has formally made a career choice AND is client aware of local Labor market information?

- **Skill Enhancement**: Does client want/need training?

- **Job Search**: Does client know how to look for work or need help to seek work?

Using the Medicine Wheel, Determine Needs In The Four Employability Dimensions

"I saw the angel in the marble and I just chiseled till I set him free."—Michelangelo

Second Phase

Part e) Clarify the four quadrants of the medicine wheel: clients' edu-cation/training (head), emotional issues (heart) such as the job loss cycle, etc., clients' skills and abilities (hands) and take note of values and beliefs expressed by clients from the things they say during the interview (home's influence on them) including their values in relation to the employment difficulty or barrier that has been identified. (Clients may not want to leave home to train in another city or to take a job because of family.)

Part f) Clarify what resources clients bring to help deal with the needs barriers identified in Part e) in light of what they possess personally and what is available in the community. Recognize limitations that exist within clients and the community as these may be barriers to employment.

The Medicine Wheel is used to clarify employment needs in the four employability dimensions: *Employment Maintenance, Career Decision Making, Skill Enhancement and Job Search.* Without such clarification, finding appropriate solutions is impossible.

The following will demonstrate how to utilize the four quadrants of the Medicine Wheel in clarifying needs in each of the four employability dimensions, beginning with Job Maintenance:

1. Clarifying Job Maintenance

HEAD

When employment issues exist clients often uses the words "I think", "I know" and makes assumptions based on their own perceptions of the employment issue. They are often immature and may or may not be well educated and do not understand it is their "**attitude**" that holds them back. They "think" they do not have an alcohol or drug problem, they "know" what employers want and may "know" our jobs better than we do. They often feel they can do no wrong and blame others for their shortcomings. These may include those who are slipping into an unhealthy lifestyle where their personalities are deteriorating.

HEART

When employment issues exist clients may be nervous, fearful and anxious, or the exact opposite … bold, living on the edge by taking foolish risks and seeming to be fearless. If afraid, they will feel threatened by everything and be highly emotional, apt to cry and abandon the counseling session because of being overly sensitive to the counselor. They feel powerless and at the mercy of fate.

Other clients may be angry and threatening to the counselor. They are unable to accept any suggestions, feel they are being criticized and will storm out of counseling sessions feeling insulted by the counselor. These clients like to exercise their power inappropriately and may bully others to get their way.

Both kinds of clients are insecure and need help to **control their emotions**. In both cases, the counselor must reassure clients that they will help them to deal with <u>employment issues</u>. These people may require professional counseling assistance to overcome their barriers to employment.

HANDS

When employment issues exist, the most common way to identify them in this dimension is to request information about any job loss, incomplete schooling or training courses. The personality may be deteriorating because of substance abuse, or other poor behaviors (theft, dishonesty, gambling, etc.). This deterioration may also show itself in negligence, lack of attention to jobs, courses, and a lack of priority to the activities required of the client. This may overlap into attitudinal problems (head) and poor values or irrational beliefs (home).

Complications exist when the client believes his/her detrimental behavior is outside their control. If this is the case, the client may need a referral to help him/her deal with it (AADAC, etc.).

HOME

When employment issues exist clients will be bound to their own values and beliefs system (<u>there is no right or wrong in client's values or belief systems</u>) and the counselor must never try to change these. However, **belief systems resulting in assumptions may compel clients to take either rational or irrational actions**. A common example of an irrational assumption (belief) is the time worn cliché, "ignorance is bliss," where clients avoid learning about or facing unpleasant topics believing what they don't know can't hurt them.

Another common assumption/belief is to always prepare for the worst (just in case) and then to expect it. There are many such irrational assumptions. Sometimes they are called superstitions which compel people to do things to avoid the "evil eye," so to speak. Counselors need to be on the alert for clients who do things that do not seem to make sense, or if their reason for doing or not doing something seems irrational. The counselor's role is to identify these behaviors and help the client to see the influence of their beliefs on themselves. This is not done by telling the client about the consequences but by asking the client to try to foresee the consequences of the belief or assumption on the client's employment prospects.

Similarly, environment and upbringing impart a system of values to clients that may block their progress. Again, values are not right or wrong, they just are. It is enough to try to help clients see the impact of their values on them. Values may be "terminal" resembling goals (wealth, happiness, etc.) or "instrumental" (how goals are achieved (honesty, courage, at all costs …). In sports, a saying is "it is not winning or losing but how the game was played." However, some want a win at any cost. These values also govern behavior.

An example is when clients refuse to leave their home on a reserve to find work as computer analysts even though there are no opportunities for this type of work in the home area. This probably stems from the belief that the family and traditional home is most valuable so the client would be reluctant to leave. It is enough to discuss the impact of this belief on clients and ensure they understand the consequences (no jobs available so either move or find other types of work).

Another example illustrating the context or environment in which clients were raised includes those raised in boarding schools and leaving those institutions with values and beliefs acquired as a result of their experiences there. These may hinder clients' future progress and impact on their employment decisions.

Again, under no circumstances should there be any attempt to change beliefs or values. The only people who can do that if need be, are the owners of those values and beliefs—the clients. If the values/beliefs are found to be barriers to their prospects for employment, clients may require professional counseling and should be referred out for assistance.

2. Clarifying Career Decision Making

HEAD

When career decision making issues exist clients may not have enough education to undertake the career of their choice so that upgrading becomes necessary. Clients may assume they know everything about the career of their choice where in fact they might not be aware of the training that is necessary or of the demand for that type of work in the local labor market, or of the profile of the occupation. They may not have rationalized whether or not they could make a living doing the chosen job. Working conditions need to be considered by clients before making a career decision.

HEART

When employment issues exist clients may lack enough desire to undertake a stated career choice. This may be because they have been told by others to "be this or that," or the type of job they think they should do is an old career choice and no longer appealing. As well, they may not have been exposed to different options that fit in with their current interests. Clients may not have properly considered their aptitudes in making a career choice (for example, their love of cooking). Their emotional responses to career opportunities must be considered before settling on a career choice. Clients may have been pushed into a job because "their uncle had an opening" and so think they must continue with this kind of work. They may be making a career choice at a time when they are discouraged, upset or under pressure to find a job quickly that will pay enough to support them. (Single parents are often in this dilemma.) It is important to help clients see past the current emergency and do what is necessary to enter a field of work that will be satisfying for the long term. Also, personality and health impacts on career decision-making and it is important to spend enough time in this area so that clients will be able to come to satisfying career decisions.

HANDS

When employment issues exist negative previous work experiences may impact on clients' decisions regarding the kind of career they may choose. Their skills and talents will also impact on their decisions. (Example: likes to do wood carving even though not formally trained). Clients' experience in doing similar work, skills and talents as well as their physical capacity to perform the chosen career needs to be considered before settling on career choices.

Clients' abilities should be considered in choosing a career and if there are problems in this area, clients need to be encouraged to reconsider the career choice. (This often relates to clients who are physically unable to undertake certain types of work. Often people with back problems will change laboring occupations for other work that is just as painful for their backs.) If there is some doubt about clients' abilities to perform jobs medical assessments from a doctor may be required to ensure clients will be able to carry out the physical duties of certain jobs.

HOME

When employment issues exist the context/environment in which clients make a career decision needs to be considered. Recent job loss or other losses (death, finances, etc.) may skew the thinking of clients. Their values may prevent them from seriously considering certain types of work such as dealer at a casino. No effort should be made to try to change clients' value systems and such jobs should be considered unsuitable even if they come up high on the list of appropriate occupations, given their interests.

Beliefs have a similar impact on career decisions and if clients believe certain jobs would not be good for them, the counselor can only present occupational profiles for them to consider as well as labor market information to try to show them that certain jobs might be suitable. Under no circumstances should the counselor try to convince clients to make career choices contrary to their beliefs. An example of this kind of choice would be to ask a Jehovah's Witness to take emergency medical technician or nursing assistant training when it could involve giving patients blood transfusions. The upbringing of clients may also impact on career decisions. An example is someone who had a problematic childhood and now wants to help people by becoming a counselor. This individual does not consider the fact that he/she may not really be suited to counsel others because of issues impacting on his/her personality.

Clients' context/environment, values, beliefs and upbringing all impact on their career choices and need to be considered when making a career decision.

3. Clarifying Skill Enhancement

HEAD

When employment issues exist clients may find they need upgrading before training for their chosen careers can be undertaken. The type of course being considered is also important—is it mostly text-book study or is it "hands on" learning? Clients will have a preference that will impact on success. Knowledge, especially of the occupation and industry, will have a bearing on how well clients do in the training. Clients must establish a rationale for taking the particular course that covers duration, costs, choice of institution/trainers, accessibility, certification, etc.. Also, clients must consider their own aptitudes for learning and study and decide whether or not they are capable of succeeding in the course being offered.

Clients must have enough knowledge about the training and the career choice to have confidence that they will succeed in the training.

HEART

When employment issues exist clients will not show much enthusiasm for the course and will consider it a chore that has to be done before getting a job. They will not be looking forward to the training with pleasure. It will be important to discuss their feelings about the course before recommending training. Part of this lack of enthusiasm may be because they must commit to attending classes on a regular basis. Past history of attending school, work or other training may point out a problem in this area that needs to be addressed through life skills training before recommending clients to training. Some clients look for funding because they need an income and feel this is an easy way to get it. They don't really care what course they take. This is a sign of an unhealthy personality and indicative of other problems in other dimensions that need to be addressed before training is considered. Even if clients were to succeed in the training (if approved for funding), the value of the learning would be undermined by lack of real motivation to take advantage of the learning available.

The initiatives clients have already carried out influence their career choices. It is important to ascertain with clients that these accomplishments will lead to appropriate career choices and not to give them undue weight if they do not. (Example: making widgets when there is no market for them).

Clients' emotional responses and commitment to the proposed training will play a major role in whether or not they succeed.

HANDS

When employment issues exist clients will have difficulty in creating and committing to action plans for training. Clients must be led to assess their own experience, skills, talents, and abilities that apply to the career and subsequent training. They may need to look into transferring existing certification credits to the course they are undertaking. The counselor should support and encourage them as they implement their action plan and throughout the duration of the course to ensure they are meeting course objectives.

HOME

When employment issues exist, clients will talk about problems at home (financial, childcare, etc.) that will make it hard for them to attend the course regularly. These are warning signs that their home life is not conducive to taking on the commitment of a training course. Clients may not consider the course as a valuable learning opportunity and may delay start dates, etc., demonstrating a lack of commitment to the training and not properly valuing the opportunity. They may not have faith (belief) that the training will open opportunities for the kind of work they seek. This may point to a problem in decision making (in an earlier dimension) indicating dissatisfaction with a career choice. Some clients will have "baggage" from quitting school, jobs, and other courses that may "cast a cloud" on the course being considered at this time. The counselor needs to satisfy him/herself that the clients have changed since then and will not abandon this learning opportunity.

It is only when personal issues are resolved and the counselor agrees that clients are fully prepared to go to training, that the counselor should be recommending the training.

4. Clarifying Job Search

HEAD

When employment issues exist clients will not know how to search for work in their chosen occupations. Clients will need to be made aware of the standard techniques of finding work in their industries. They may have erroneous assumptions about seeking work that need to be corrected. Clients need to create a plan for work search so that they incorporate the best techniques for finding work in the industry, for the specific occupation.

This plan should cover efficiency, economy and effectiveness to make the most of the job search effort. The results of the job search need to be analyzed (perhaps with the help of the counselor) to establish the reasons why the search may not have been successful. These findings should give rise to changes in the job search approach. Clients need to have a sound knowledge of how to search for jobs in their occupations. Targeted wage subsidy may help to get the client's "foot in the employer's door," providing there are absolutely no other needs to be resolved.

HEART

When employment issues exist, clients will not be enthusiastic about looking for work and feel it is a chore or even frightening. They may have negative attitudes about employers because of past interactions. This must be explored to identify potential issues that need to be addressed by clients. Their commitment to finding work may not be genuine i.e. they are being sent out the door to find work by a mother or wife but would rather stay home.

This lack of motivation also needs attention to identify the factors that are dampening their enthusiasm. Searching for work may cause fear and nervousness that requires clients to overcome such internal feelings which render job search a nightmare for them. The counselor needs to identify and help clients address these fears through plans and practice.

A lack of enthusiasm for job search or even fear and nervousness needs to be addressed before sending clients on work search. Otherwise, they will only compound their feelings of failure and rejection.

HANDS

When employment issues exist, clients will be vague about the activities they undertook to find work. They should be asked for details about these activities. As well, they should describe the employer's response giving quotes where possible. Therefore, a job search record is very important, as it will serve to analyze clients' efforts and identify problems they may not be aware of regarding job search skills and abilities. Clients can then plan on how to acquire the needed skills (interviews) and practice them.

Clients may be busily contacting 10 employers each day without securing work. In contrast, other clients may only contact one employer and succeed in finding a job. It is important to remember that it is the quality of the contact and not the quantity that matters.

The job search record will also reveal issues that may be outside the control of clients (age, disability, discrimination, etc.). Counselors may need to resort to other methods in assisting such clients by using specialized services to help place them into employment.

Vagueness about job search indicates a lack of enthusiasm and/or a lack of responsibility and commitment to carrying out an efficient job search.

HOME

When employment issues exist, they may be either within the clients' locus of control or outside their control. Those issues clients can control include their values and beliefs, although these are extremely hard to change. (Clients should never be asked to change their values and beliefs.) They may arbitrarily cut themselves out of a large part of the job market because the demand is not on the reserve or near to where they live. Clients may also restrict themselves to working only for Aboriginal employers. Other such beliefs may reduce clients' chances of finding work and the counselor's duty is to ensure clients appreciate this without debasing their values or beliefs. As well, clients may have brought localized job search methods which are inappropriate in seeking work in a bigger urban labor market. Efforts to get a job must be reviewed in detail to ensure clients are using the best possible techniques for the local labor market. (Conversely, when urbanites who are used to doing a formal job search move to a small labor market, they may need to adapt to less formal and more personal job search approaches because these are now the norm.)

Issues outside the control of clients include the state of the local labor market, in particular, the demand. Clients cannot change the industrial demand for workers so the solution is to choose jobs that provide them with a reasonable chance to become self-sufficient. Searching for a job where there is little or no demand will be fruitless unless clients change their occupations to those that are in demand.

Job search issues faced by the client may or may not be within their control so that counselors need to lead them in taking notice of the problems and address them if possible. Counselors are responsible for ensuring clients are aware of local supply and demand by providing such information through Labor Market Information (LMI) sessions before they make career decisions. If their career decisions have already been made, and they are in a low demand occupation, clients should be helped to the extent possible to find work given the poor prospects they face or by making a new career decision to find work that is in demand.

Because counselors do not own their clients' problems, they do not have the power to solve them, only the power to <u>use their own and organizational resources to help clients</u> reach their own solutions. Therefore, one of the main goals of counseling is to help clients see their employment issues clearly and understand that they alone have the power to deal with them with the assistance of counselors.

Ownership of issues relates closely to locus of control. It is important (as the well-known Serenity Prayer suggests) to understand when it is reasonable to drive personal change for oneself and when one must wait for something external to change before proceeding. Therefore, a balanced approach is most desirable.

At the end of the clarification process, the counselor should review the clients' original constraint statement and revise it based on the new understandings that have been reached as a result of the clarification. Clients need to agree that the constraints identified are valid and need to be resolved. This will lead to a "plan" for resolving these constraints.

Third Phase—Steps for Action Planning

"It's better to forge ahead and make mistakes than look back and go nowhere."—Author unknown

Part g) Create contingency statements and establish counseling goals. Each of the four employability dimensions may have a counseling goal if there are needs in that dimension.

The ultimate counseling goals are for clients to either achieve self sufficiency in one or more or the four employability dimensions and/or to find suitable work or self employment. However, counseling goals also relate to the main accomplishments planned for clients in a dimension that will resolve all employment difficulties in that area. (Examples: complete training as a legal secretary for Skill Enhancement, make an appropriate career decision for Career Decision Making, update safety tickets through training to be able to keep or find a job under Skill Enhancement, etc..)

Counseling goals must be **"SMART"** according to Paul J. Meyers. They must be: "**S**pecific", "**M**easurable", "**A**greed", "**R**ealistic" and "**T**imed."

A SMART goal for career decision making is for clients to decide on careers (specific, measurable, agreed, and realistic) by the end of next week (timed). Alternatively, in Skill Enhancement a goal might be to complete and pass the office administration course as agreed to by clients and become certified by the course end week (date).

There are usually four reasons why counseling goals are not achieved:

1.   The steps toward achieving the goal need to be changed (courses cancelled, etc.).

2.   The counseling goal is no longer suitable or was not suitable in the first place. (This might relate to clients who find they are incapable of performing jobs they used to do or want to do as a result of health deterioration, age, or other barriers).

3.   Clients found employment before counseling goal was achieved.

4.   Clients abandoned their action plans.

In these cases, revised counseling goals will be established if necessary and plans to achieve them will continue to be implemented by clients, or case files will be closed while clients are employed or have abandoned the plan. When/if they return the counseling goals will be reviewed and modified as needed.

When all counseling goals have been achieved but clients are still unemployed, they may be deemed "self-sufficient" because there are no goals left to be achieved in any of the four employability dimensions. These clients are able to deal with all of their employment needs independently. Specifically, these are clients who:

1.   Have made a career decision;

2.   Have acquired/demonstrated required skills and knowledge;

3.   Are actively and independently engaged in a planned job search; and

4.   Are active and independent in job maintenance skills during employment.

Counseling goals (there may be more than one counseling goal for one dimension) are a natural product of contingency statements. Therefore, it is important to structure these statements so that the counseling goal emerges naturally in the words of the client. Contingency statements have two parts and relate directly to the constraint statement made during the clarification process done previously. Contingency statements break the inertia of the constraint statement and begin movement towards a goal. The first part of the contingency statement turns the old constraint statement into a positive from a negative tone. The last part of the contingency statement can be considered the counseling goal for that dimension as demonstrated below:

Here is a chart showing how the constraint statement leads into the contingency statement and the counseling goal:

Constraint Statement:	
"No one will hire me because my safety tickets are expired."	
Contingency Statement:	**Counseling Goal:**
If I want to find work -	then I must –
Constraint Statement:	
"Since I was hurt I can't do my old job anymore."	
Contingency Statement:	**Counseling Goal:**
If I want a job I could do given my back injury –	then I must -

The client identifies the counseling goal by completing the contingency statement. (What employability dimensions would contain the above goals?)

Each action plan under each employability dimension where there are needs identified for the client, must show a counseling goal. The contingency statement, as a means of identifying the counseling goal, is presented clearly for agreement, confirmation or further clarification. Each goal should be written in the "SMART" format for each dimension.

The constraint statement made earlier by the client (negative—indicating a "stalled position") is changed to a positive action statement as a lead-in to the counseling goal for that dimension and to the subsequent steps in an action plan.

The new statement contains the "contingency" or "possibility" usually starting with the words "If I want … (achieving a desirable state)", and ending with what action must be taken by the client: "then I must…." The main action to be taken under each dimension will usually become a counseling goal for that dimension.

Part h) Generate, validate and prioritize options with the client by choosing the best, second best, etc. and recording the steps to be taken to achieve the goal in that dimension.

The counselor now helps the client to generate options to satisfy the counseling goal for that employability dimension. This is where the client's resources, the employment counselor's resources, the organization's resources, the community partner's resources must all be identified and considered. The counselor takes this opportunity to explain the kinds of programs and services available through the organization and outside the organization.

A good method of generating a variety of options for issues identified in each employability dimension is to participate with the client in a "brain storm" session. Here are some guidelines for having a brainstorming session with a client:

1. Advise the client to put forward all ideas without deciding if the ideas are good or bad.

2. Tell the client we are looking for as many ideas as possible and to include his/her wishes and desires in the ideas put forward no matter how impossible they might seem.

3. Inform the client of the resources available from the organization (programs and services) and from community partners.

4. Avoid giving clients solutions (programs or services that might help); rather, wait for the client to find the best solution him/herself.

5. Counselors may bring forward any of the client's ideas expressed while clarifying needs.

6. List client's ideas during brainstorming but do not evaluate them.

7. Repeat the contingency statement often to spur the client into identifying other possibilities.

Validating and prioritizing options is another way to say "decision making." Often this is done without adequate consideration of the options available. It is not enough to have the client choose what he/she thinks are the best because clients will not systematically assess options before selecting one that <u>seems</u> good. A good approach is to use a decision grid that we learned about earlier to assess different options that emerge during brainstorming. Different actions might be taken by the client to achieve the desired state so as many options as possible should be generated through brainstorming to have a good variety from which the client may choose.

The decision grid is a systematic way of exploring the advantages and disadvantages of the options having regard to what the client says is important to him/her. Assigning weight to the criteria is also a way of reflecting the client's priorities in considering the options. The criteria or its weight may be changed after the client sees the impact of his/her demands on the options that once seemed appropriate. The counselor should be flexible in guiding the client through this exercise of decision-making. Often, it will serve as an eye opener to the client about what is or is not really important to them when considering suitable jobs or other employment issues.

Although is it recognized that the decision grid takes time to do, counselors are encouraged to use it when, in their opinion, the client is unsure of his/her desires or has made some hasty decisions that may not be appropriate.

Part i) Together with the client, make the action plan to achieve goals in each employability dimension. An action plan is a blue print for positive change. It is wise to remember how people perceive change:

- Clients may feel a sense of loss

- Clients tend to feel as though they are "going it alone"

- As change starts to happen, they feel uncomfortable and want to go back to the way things used to be

- As change continues, they may become frustrated and start to resist it

- As soon as change is not being led i.e. by the counselor, clients may abandon plans and revert to their original state

Therefore, before starting an action plan for change, counselors should help the client clearly envision what that change will look like for him/her and what benefits it will bring. This is done through discussion of improvements to the client's life after succeeding in their plan for change. This is their motivation to plan and carry out the process of change. The counselor needs to be sure the client can envision the end result in order to help him/her to commit to the planned change process through the action plan.

The action plan establishes the first step toward making change happen. It is here that the client may display resistance and will need to be motivated so that she/he will commit to making changes. Key to ensuring clients remain motivated is to ensure the steps are clearly understood and are kept to simple tasks as much as possible. Complicated activities will put the client off and lead to failure. Therefore, if you require research for a career study or to learn about labor market information locally, agree with the client exactly what information is needed and why. Then advise the client where to look for it (web sites, libraries, LMI sessions, Career Cruising software, etc.). Provide him/her with some printed format that specifies the exact issues to be researched. This will then be used for recording the information as a result of the agreement you have reached.

In all cases, the action plan should show WHO, WHAT, WHERE, HOW and WHEN about the activities to be done. Clients then sign the action plan to show they agree and are given a copy to serve as a reference document for what they are to undertake. Counselors may also need to accomplish certain tasks and they will also record these initiatives in the client's action plan. If outside partners are to be involved, their identities need to be recorded and appointments made by the counselor with the client present to ensure dates and times are suitable for all parties.

Action planning, therefore, involves the client and counselor agreeing on appropriate steps that will lead to the client achieving the counseling goal. These steps are recorded in the action plan to provide a record of the activities agreed to by the client and the counselor. These steps will be carried out under the case management of the counselor who will assist as needed and monitor the client's progress throughout. If the client encounters problems in carrying out these steps the counselor will assist the client and motivate him/her to continue, as mentioned.

Fourth Phase—Case Management & Results

Part j) It is after the action plan has been created that case management begins. Each step of the action plan is case managed by the counselor to assess the progress toward change and to identify if the changes achieved by the client require a review of the remaining action steps to re-establish relevance. The outcome of each step of the action plan must be documented on the client's file. An amended action plan may be needed to address new difficulties encountered by the client.

The counselor is required to maintain control of the file until the client no longer needs assistance and the file is documented to that effect. Therefore, after each visit by the client, there should be some indication of when the client is going to return to see the counselor to report on the outcome of the steps taken in the action plan. The file is put into a pending state with a "bring forward" date entered to the appropriate case manager. This will ensure the file is reconsidered at the proper future date. At that time, the outcomes of the previous steps are reviewed and the future steps in the action plan are assessed to ensure they continue to be relevant to the client's goal. If not, the action plan will be renegotiated with the client, incorporating new steps that are more appropriate.

If the client does not report at the required time, the case manager will contact the client to determine the outcome of the steps that were taken by the client. This activity may comprise "follow-up" activity on the part of the case manager.

Part k) Ideally follow-up occurs after all the steps of the action plan have been completed to see if the client found work and/or if client is self-sufficient. (Client has no more needs or has learned how to satisfy his/her own needs in each employability dimension and does not need any further assistance from the counselor). Otherwise, follow-up may begin early after the client fails to report back to the counselor at the pre-arranged time.

Many Aboriginal employment organizations sign agreements with government funders that require results in terms of "found work or self employment" as part of their accountability or obligation. Therefore follow-up assumes high priority. Finding work is an easily measurable result which, when entered into the organizational data base/client tracking system, yields a "credit". Measuring "self-sufficiency" is more tenuous and needs to relate back to the needs that were identified and the counseling goals that were set. The counselor, together with the client, must decide if needs were met and goals achieved, even if work or self-employment did not occur. The critical question for follow-up is "what else can be done to help the client find work?" If there seems to be nothing more to be done and the client feels he/she is capable of finding work on his/her own, the file may be closed. Otherwise, the client will be re-assessed to determine what new needs exist to be dealt with under the appropriate employability dimension.

Follow-up is usually started with clients when the action plan is completed and they are looking for work, either under supervision or independently. A period of 30 days to find work is usually allowed before follow-up is undertaken. If the first follow-up contact shows clients did not find work, another contact is made after 60 days and again, just before 90 days lapses to allow registering the found work credit into the computer tracking system. (There may be arbitrary limits set out for accepting inputs into tracking systems. Inputs made more than 90 days after the completion of skill enhancement intervention do not count as a bona fide result for the purpose of an Aboriginal/federal agreement. It would be wise to consult with Service Canada consultants to ascertain the current policy.) When clients find work, this is entered into the computer tracking system, ensuring that all needs in any dimensions are shown to have been satisfied.

Often, project sponsors place their graduates into employment so it is essential to ensure good communication exists between counselors and project partners to record employment outcomes for clients who have found employment.

It is during this 90-day period of job search that clients may be considered for assistance to help them gain entry into jobs for which they may not be given consideration due to lack of experience or job maintenance issues. A targeted wage subsidy provided to an employers may help offset wage costs and provide an incentive to hire.

In other cases, clients may disappear without completing their action plans. If all efforts to contact them are unsuccessful, and there is no forwarding address, their files will be closed and the status will be recorded as "unknown." This does not result in a good outcome for the organization and counselors should ensure alternative addresses/contacts are identified and well documented.

Examples—Show me!

1. A client-centered approach may be achieved during a group interview session if the session is designed to be interactive with the clients. The facilitator poses open-ended questions to the clients encouraging them to participate, there are assistants circulating to help with the completion of forms and clients are encouraged to be active during the sessions.

2. The client record shows the client said, "I can't do laboring work anymore because my doctor says my knees are not strong enough." The constraint statement is: "My doctor said I can't do laboring anymore." The contingency statement is: "If I want to find suitable work I must change my occupation from laboring." The employability dimension is career decision-making. The smart counseling goal is:

Specific: To change my occupation.

Measurable: To change my occupation to one that is suitable (such as administrative assistant, etc.).

Agreed: Client, doctor and employment counselor agree this occupation is suitable given client's attributes under head: has appropriate education to enter training; heart: wants to do this occupation; hands: occupation is suitable given the client's physical limitations/abilities; home: client's past experience, values and beliefs do not conflict with this occupation.

Realistic: The chosen occupational goal is realistic (ie. brain surgeon might not be realistic given the amount of education the client will need before entering medical school …).

Timed: To attend a session booked for "next Monday" to make an appropriate career decision.

Summary and Key Points—What is most important about this issue?

Good interview patterns combined with communication skills utilizing the four employability dimensions and the Medicine Wheel, will lead to professional interviewing and accurate needs identification. Using the constraint statements to develop "SMART" counseling goals and generate appropriate options for satisfying employment needs will help to create a realistic action plan to enable clients to reach their employment goal.

Self-Test Questions—How well do I understand this?

1. What is a "client-centered" approach to interviewing clients?

2. What are the four phases of a client interview?

3. Describe in order, the four quadrants of a Medicine Wheel, as they would be used to explore needs in the four employability dimensions.

4. Write the constraint statement for the following: "I have no baby sitter or money for child care to allow me to look for work."

5. What is the counseling goal for #4 above?

6. Write the counseling goal in #5 in "SMART" terms.

7. Why is it important to ensure follow-up, for the purpose of taking a credit for "found work" under an Aboriginal Human Resources Development Agreement with the government, is completed before 90 days after the last funded date lapses?

14

Case Managing, Documentation & Client Tracking

Chapter Goal—To use a balanced approach in monitoring client progress through the action plan (case management) including timely entries into the computer tracking system.

Background—Important issues about this topic follow.
Important issues relate to the employment counselor's responsibilities for ensuring a client is making good progress through his/her action plan. This means there should never be a time when an employment counselor is not aware of the activities in which a client is engaged. As well, if any activities become inappropriate, it is up to the employment counselor to discuss changes with the client as soon as possible. The action plan must be in active status at all times when the client is being assisted by the employment counselor.

Motivation—Why do you need to understand this?

It is important to recognize signs of resistance to action plan steps, or loss of motivation to continue, early on, in order to help the client regain commitment to employment goals. In identifying such problems it might become evident that the client's employment goals are changing, in which case it will be necessary to re-explore the job maintenance and career decision-making dimensions through the lens of the Medicine Wheel.

Presentation—How does it work?

Case managing a client means that an employment counselor will retain control of the client's action plan, keeping the hard copy and computer file up to date by referring the client to appropriate interventions agreed upon with the client. The file will be reviewed by the employment counselor through the "bring forward" system ensuring the file comes back for re-examination immediately after the expected completion dates of the planned interventions. The employment counselor/case manager is responsible for recording the outcomes of the interventions and together with the client, adjusting the next steps of the action plan, if necessary. This case management continues until the client finds work, or until the client is deemed self-sufficient and can look for work on his/her own, or the client abandons the action plan for various reasons (moves away, etc.).

Case management always ends with "follow-up" to determine if the client needs any further service, if he/she has found work or self-employment or to find out the reasons why the client is no longer seeking the organization's services (see Chapter 13). These reasons are recorded on the client's hard copy and computer file. Even when the client cannot be contacted the file will be notated, "unknown."

The following functions constitute case management:

1. Creating a file or reactivating an existing file and assigning an employment counselor as case manager;

2. Identifying any barriers to employment and making appropriate referrals to specialists, if necessary;

3. Assessing the client's employment needs under the four employability dimensions and making appropriate referrals to address these needs;

4. Discussing employment needs with the client and agreeing on how each intervention will be carried out;

5. Confirming a mutual understanding of what "success" will be for each intervention undertaken by the client;

6. Discussing how the employment counselor/case manager will participate in each intervention through monitoring, measuring success and getting client feedback on the quality of the intervention;

7. Reviewing next steps for relevancy after each intervention is completed;

8. Adjusting action plans as required;

9. Continuing with the action plan until either the client has achieved self-sufficiency or has found work or self-employment;

10. Setting next meeting dates;

11. Bringing the file forward for each meeting with the client to document the file and note another "bring forward" date, unless the client is no longer expected to report to the employment counselor/case manager; and

12. Entering data into the computer tracking system to indicate needs have been satisfied in any dimensions.

Note that many interventions performed by contracted service providers have their own case managers performing functions on behalf of the organization. It is still the responsibility of the organization to make suitable arrangements for an exchange of information between the contracted case managers and the organization's own employment counselors/case managers about the client's progress so that the client may be "tracked" through the intervention.

Tracking a client's activities means documenting all undertakings initiated by the client or the case manager, onto the client's hard copy and computer file. Each stage of the client flow is tracked and the progress/outcomes documented. This history is the "track" of the client through the client flow in the service organization. This track allows others to pick up and continue the client's action plan if it becomes interrupted. The track will also include contracted case manager's reports on the client's progress through contracted interventions. It will be the responsibility of the organization's employment counselor/case manager to input such tracking data received from the contractors onto the client's hard copy and computer files.

A computer file should contain notes under all four of the employability dimensions on how needs were resolved. "Comments" sections should cover any special considerations or decisions made by the client and the case manager. If tracking has been effective, anyone picking up the client's files can become familiar with the client's case and continue on with it, as mentioned previously.

Tracking forms include all documentation forms used by the organization, a record of all interventions, the client's progress and the outcomes, and finally the follow-up and results achieved.

Examples—Show me!

1. The client is scheduled to attend a three-day session (offered by partners) in order to make a career decision. The employment counselor notates the action plan to this effect and selects a "bring forward" date two days after the scheduled completion date of the career decision-making session, as the time of the next meeting with the client. After the three-day session, the partner (contracted to do career decision-making) advises the employment counselor of the results of the session by email and when the client returns to meet with the counselor, this decision is discussed.

    When both the client and the employment counselor agree that the career decision made is sound, the file and computer tracking system will be notated that a career decision was made with the name of the occupation. The interview will proceed into the skill enhancement dimension to ascertain what education and training are required by the client for the selected occupation. Once again the file (hard copy and computer) are notated with the results of the interview. An employment goal (in 'SMART' terms) together with an action plan is prepared by the client with the counselor's help, outlining the steps that will be taken to achieve that goal.

2. The training institution contacts the employment counselor advising that the client has missed three days of classes. The employment counselor contacts the client and learns there has been a death in the immediate family but that the client is now back in class. The employment counselor determines that the client will receive allowances for that period (instead of making deductions) in accordance with the organizational training policy on bereavement. The hard copy file and the computer tracking file are notated to that effect.

Summary and Key Points—What is most important about this issue?

Once an employment counselor accepts a client for programs and services, there should never be a time when that client is unsupervised. The employment counselor should know on which steps of the action plan the client is currently working. This hands-on supervision should continue until the client either finds work or is considered self-sufficient with no outstanding needs.

Self-Test Questions—How well do I understand this?

1. Why is continued supervision of the implementation of an action plan so important to monitoring progress?

2. The client returns to the employment counselor after successfully completing upgrading to a grade 10 level and tells the counselor that she no longer wants to be a personal care assistant. Instead she wants to be a bookkeeper but she needs grade 12 math and English. What are the main things the employment counselor must do to document the file?

15

Quality and Competencies for Effective Employment Counseling

Chapter Goal—To achieve balance in the delivery of quality employment services, having regard for acceptable standard of competency in employment counseling.

Background—Important issues about this topic follow.
Important issues in employment counseling relate to the delivery of services and programs to clients. Therefore, it is critical to understand what "service" comprises. Service must not be confused with "goods." A service is usually a "deed, act, or performance."

Motivation—Why do you need to understand this?

The most critical concept to understand is that, unlike a bottle of ketchup that relies on a good recipe to give it quality, the quality of a service relies entirely on the person delivering the service.

Presentation—How does it work?

The business of employment counseling requires the delivery of quality employment services. These services have the following special characteristics:

1. Heterogeneity

2. Intangibility

3. Inseparability

4. Perishability

1. What is "Heterogeneity"?

Service delivery is very different, depending on who delivers the service. Service will change from one organization to another, from one client to another and from day to day. Therefore we can say service delivery is heterogeneous.

The quality of the service will depend directly on how it is delivered by the person. If that person is sick, angry or frustrated, the service will be affected by the mood of the deliverer. It has been found that people using the bus system in a certain city unconsciously respond to the bus driver's mood and if he is happy that day, they too are happy and in a good mood ... or just the opposite if the driver is moody and sullen.

In trying to control the final product (service being delivered to clients), it is important for managers and staff to maintain a consistent routine in the office that promotes a maximum comfort level for those delivering services. Staff delivering services should be very familiar with processes used to deliver services so that they can focus on the needs of the client before them and relate to the client in the best possible way. Personal problems must be kept separate from the office environment. This is difficult to do but as a service deliverer, it is crucial not only to the counselor's reputation with clients, but also to the reputation of the organization. To clients the counselor is the "face" of the organization. Therefore, any interaction with clients—both positive and negative—will reflect on the entire organization.

The perception of the organization is based on <u>image</u>, <u>reputation,</u> and <u>satisfaction</u> ... **not of the organization, but of YOU!** Therefore, in order to create an outstanding organization that offers satisfying client service, each counselor must cultivate a good image and reputation to ensure client satisfaction.

2. What is Intangibility?

While a product can be seen, touched, smelled, (sampled), a service cannot as it is intangible. Services are evaluated by clients solely on how satisfying they are as an experience or on what results they help the client to achieve. Clients can only imagine what the service might be before they agree to take delivery of the service. This is why in counseling, it is important to ensure clients fully understand what the counseling relationship will be, the steps that will be undertaken (action plan as agreed to by the client) and the goals of the action plan. It is only after such initiatives are taken that the client will better understand what services are being offered and how they will help to accomplish their goals. Then the client will either "buy in" or not. Clients must have a good feeling about the counselor with whom they will work. If counselors feel that there is a problem with the relationship, they should immediately see their manager to discuss the problem and possible solutions. If the client does not want to discuss their reservations with the counselor, he/she should be referred to the manager for consultation and problem solving. A different counselor may be assigned. There may be any number of reasons (age, gender, personality clashes, etc.) why a client may feel they do not relate well to an assigned counselor and this should not be held against him/her.

Service delivery becomes an even greater challenge when the client's values, beliefs, and attitudes are contrary to the ideas being offered in the counseling services. Success, in that case, depends solely on the reputation and credibility of the service deliverer. Counselors will do well to continually strive to exemplify a good image as a role model to successfully "sell" services.

3. What is Inseparability?

When service cannot be separated from the service deliverer, this is called inseparability.

Warehouses are able to store products for months but services are immediately "consumed" as they are delivered. The client who is accepting the service is in intimate contact with the service deliverer in order to use the service. This means that everything about the service that is being delivered is focused on the moment it is delivered. A service cannot be separated from the service deliverer because they are one and the same.

Some influences on the moment that services are delivered include: the condition of the person delivering the service, the condition of the client receiving the service and the condition of the environment in which the service is being delivered. If all of these variables are in "good" condition, then it is probable that the perception of the client regarding the service delivered will be good too. The opposite will also invite a negative perception.

Many services available to clients are virtually the same as those offered by other organizations. The key is to offer services to clients that are or seem more attractive/different than those offered by others. It is not necessary that the services offered are truly different or better, but it is imperative that clients <u>perceive</u> that the services offered are different and better.

One way to discover what unique services clients want is by conducting a "client satisfaction survey." In one such survey, it was determined that clients rated privacy and security very highly when it came to dealing with their personal issues. They wanted to be sure they could trust their counselors. Therefore, a "big seller" to the client would be the counselor's transparent and straightforward adherence to client confidentiality legislation.

In attracting certain client groups for service delivery, market surveys have been done to identify where these groups are situated, geographically. This is known as "market segmentation" and has already been completed by most organizations for their market groups. However, many agencies want to attract or "target" certain priority groups, which include youth, women, etc. where special services can be provided. In all cases of targeting, the service delivery organization must keep abreast of the groups' needs and keep positioning and repositioning to plan strategies to address these needs. Therefore, continual monitoring of the groups' characteristics and surveying these clients regarding their satisfaction with services provided will point the way to making these services more attractive to the segment of clients the agency wants to serve.

4. What is Perishability?

While goods can be stored for future delivery, services cannot. This means that the quality of a service cannot be guaranteed from one day to the next in the same way that the quality of a bottle of ketchup might be assured. The quality of the service depends directly on three factors at the moment of delivery: the conditions of the service deliverer, service receiver and the environment or context under which the service is being delivered (similar to inseparability).

During periods of high demand we cannot bring out stored services to meet the demand. Instead, we must find innovative ways to deliver services to meet the demand at the exact time that the demand exists, no earlier and no later. Services, then, are on a just-in-time basis. Quality of service, especially during periods of peak demand, will either enhance the service deliverer's reputation or will destroy it. If the quality of services is lacking, consumers/clients will be certain to report this to others, further damaging the organization's credibility.

If employment counselors can confidently say that they know how to counsel clients in accordance with high standards, and if they present a good image to clients, then the competency level is consistent with the standards that follow. The following competencies, based on the "American National Employment Counseling Competencies" may be used in the Medicine Wheel approach to employment counseling to ensure high standards of service delivery:

1. **Counseling**—the ability to establish a trusting, open and beneficial relationship with each client through the use of appropriate communication skills to share information on relevant employment programs and services, and to use all four quadrants of the Medicine Wheel to help the client to establish balance through change, decision making and goal setting.

2. **Individual and Group Assessment**—the ability to assess and case manage clients' progress individually and as a group having regard to their needs, characteristics, potentials, differences and the client's own self-assessment of progress.

3. **Group Dynamics**—the ability to conduct group sessions for the purpose of informing, fact finding, documenting, assessing needs, and helping clients to make action plans for dealing with needs.

4. **Accessing and Interpreting Labor Market Information**—the ability to access, understand and interpret labor market information and job trends in order to assist clients to make career decisions and set employment goals that lead to self-sufficiency, while having regard to each client's individual profile in every quadrant of the medicine wheel.

5. **Computer Related**—The ability to coach clients on using internet and other online tools and resources such as job banks, job search and job match tools; resume writing and sharing tools; automated labor market information systems; vacancy lists including the ability to use automated computer program management tools for monitoring client progress, documentation and reporting while maintaining the confidentiality of client data.

6. **Employment Action Plan and Case Management**—the ability to assist the client to create a mutually agreeable action plan and to support the client in moving through it a step at a time, making such adjust-

ments to ensure the client progresses in a balanced way toward attaining employment goals and becoming self-sufficient.

7. **Helping Client to Find Work**—the ability to assist clients in presenting their skills and qualifications to employers and to help clients search for work. The ability to advocate on behalf of clients as required (First Nations, persons with disabilities, women, youth, etc.).

8. **Accessing Community Resources**—the ability to assist clients with identified barriers to employment and obtain the services they require to overcome them. The ability to make presentations to such community partners and participate with them in community initiatives dealing with employment, education and occupational training issues.

9. **Workload Management/Teamplayer**—the ability to work as a team member with other staff in coordinating and managing client loads, providing uninterrupted service to clients and carrying a fair share of local office duties so as to ensure a smooth operation of the employment center.

10. **Professional Development**—the ability to take the initiative to develop and maintain competencies in communication; client needs assessment; understanding demand and supply issues in the local labor market; information sharing; networking for the purposes of accessing community resources; assisting clients to achieve balance in employment-related aspects in all four quadrants of the Medicine Wheel by providing guidance, referral to community experts as required, helping clients plan and implement change, case managing clients' progress towards employment goals; and to demonstrate by example the qualities expected of a role model in this position.

11. **Ethical & Legal Issues**—the ability to comply with ethical standards developed by the employer and to be aware of the contents of relevant legislation such as the Privacy Act, The Access to Information Legislation, Labor Standards, Canadian Labor Law, The EI Act and Regulations, among other legislation.

Examples—Show me!

1. An employment counselor comes to work with a bad cold because there is no one else to replace him. Nevertheless, he is miserable and unable to deal properly with his clients. His supervisor decides he should go home

for the day and asks the receptionist to call his appointments and cancel them. The supervisor also volunteers to take those clients who are already on their way into the office. This way, he has taken steps to protect the counselor's and the organization's image, and ensured that service delivery was not compromised.

2. The employment counselor does not get along well with her fellow workers or her clients. She is always complaining about her health and takes lots of time off. She does not bother documenting her client files and dislikes using the computer so she seldom inputs anything into the tracking system. Since she has been with the organization longest, she is considered the senior counselor. The other staff and clients do not like her and her clients often stop coming to see her. She has a poor image and her counseling competencies are questionable.

3. The employment counselor is afraid to speak in front of a group of people. In order to help her over this, her co-workers bring her into group sessions where there is a firm agenda and she takes part with the help of the others in the session. Before long, she learns how to lead these sessions comfortably.

Summary and Key Points—What is most important about this issue?

Employment counselors need to understand that they are the "face" of the organization to the client. If this "face" is pleasant and helpful, clients will be more inclined to find satisfaction with the service than if the "face" is moody and impatient. As well, employment counselors must learn counseling competencies in order to deliver high quality employment counseling services.

Self-Test Questions—How well do I understand this?

1. An employment counselor lives in a small community and likes to go to the bar to drink and gamble on Saturday nights where he often meets clients. Is this a good idea or not, and why?

2. How could the list of employment counseling competencies be used in a decision grid for hiring or assessing the performance of employment counselors?

3. Why is it important for an employment counselor to know what community resources are available and how to access them?

16

Ethics, Privacy and Access to Information

Chapter Goal—To balance the protection of clients' rights to privacy with the personal values and beliefs of service delivery personnel for ethical client service.

Background—Important issues about this topic follow.
Important issues to understand are that codes of ethics are rules for the behavior of those charged with public trust to perform their duties according to acceptable standards, in an objective manner. The first rule is to avoid being put into a conflict of interest situation. The second rule, generally, is to withdraw from a position of authority or perceived authority if personal interests become involved. Federal Privacy Legislation allows employment agencies to become custodians of personal employment information that is protected from access by the public. It is important to distinguish the Federal Privacy Legislation and Access to Information Acts from any provincial legislation that may exist in order to provide a consistent approach to privacy and access for clients, and because of the Federal agreements that fund the operation of employment centers and programs.

Personal information banks (client files) are always restricted, whereas statistical reports, labor market information and other information of a non-personal nature may be accessed freely by those requesting this data. Such accessible information includes policy and procedure manuals, annual and quarterly reports, and other data except that which is expressly designated as "protected" including the procedure for filing according to social insurance numbers.

Motivation—Why do you need to understand this?

An employment counselor's personal image may be compromised when a conflict of interest situation arises, as well as that of the organization. Once lost, a trustworthy reputation is difficult to regain. In order to avoid legal difficulties an employment counselor must understand what information is private (with a restricted access) and which information is accessible to the public and how to access both types of information. In most cases open information banks are accessed without any special procedures, but in some cases permission must be requested in writing. In other situations, information is restricted for a certain number of years, (20, 30, 40, 50 years) until it is deemed appropriate to share with the public.

An example of such a case is, when after 50 years of being classified highly secret and restricted in access, the information on the Russian spy, Igor Gouzenko (who had lived in Canada) was finally opened to the public. This is probably because most of the people involved had died and the issues were obsolete.

Service Canada will have additional information on the Privacy and Access to Information Act. It is worthwhile to invite them for a visit to provide your office with the most recent information in this area and to ask for brochures to be sent to you.

Presentation—How does it work?

It is suggested that employment counselors adhere to the following code of ethics in the administration of their duties. (This code is generally based on a proposal made by Wm. E Schultz):

1. With respect to employment counseling competencies and the Medicine Wheel, an employment counselor will use appropriate counseling tools and resources (in particular the four employability dimensions approach, labor market information, community networks, etc.) to create positive relationships that will help clients overcome employment barriers and address their employment needs.

2. Although information surrounding the client is protected by the provisions of the Federal Privacy Act, it may be released to proper authorities

if: clients threaten to harm themselves or others; written authorization is provided by the client for such information to be shared; instructed by the courts to divulge such information; or the employment counselor needs to consult with other professionals about the client's situation.

3. Before an employment counselor embarks on assisting clients, they must be advised about the interview process to be used, including the purpose, goals and methods. Such an explanation should include reference to action plans, client's rights and obligations and how partners may be asked to assist in dealing with barriers and employment needs.

4. Employment counselors must strive for balance in each quadrant of the Medicine Wheel so as to achieve good values and belief systems from the home quadrant. They are expected to have adequate education, (head quadrant), be impartial and objective to all types of clients (heart quadrant), as well as learn appropriate counseling skills to deliver high quality counseling to clients (hand quadrant). They must be aware of and comply with the Canadian Human Rights Act.

5. Employment counselors must be aware of community resources and refer clients out when there is a need for other professional interventions. Employment counselors are restricted to dealing with employment issues and must avoid trying to assist clients in areas beyond their mandated capacity. If in doubt, clients should be referred out to professionals who will assess and address the client's needs.

6. Employment counselors should be prepared to offer group counseling services ensuring the objectives of the group meeting are clearly stated and the process to be used specifically outlined. Client privacy regarding the information being gathered as a result of the group interaction must be kept confidential. As well, the employment counselor is responsible for protecting the clients from any type of bullying or threatening behavior from other clients.

7. Organizational staff and agents are not authorized to perform research except to survey the satisfaction of clients with services and to perform follow-up activities. Because of the intricacies involved with designing tests to achieve promote valid research results, only qualified researchers are permitted to conduct research. In that event, all research subjects

should be informed of the purpose of the study. Participation in research must be voluntary. The researcher is also responsible for:

a.   The welfare of the research subjects;

b.   The anonymity of research subjects; and

c.   The accurate reporting of research.

8.   Only certified test administrators are allowed to administer certain tests. If qualified, an employment counselor provides adequate orientation and information on standardized tests so that the results may be placed in proper perspective with other relevant information. The effects of socio-economic, cultural, and ethnic factors on standardized tests must be acknowledged.

9.   When computers are used as part of the service for clients, the employment counselor must ensure that:

a.   The client understands how to use computer applications;

b.   The computer application is appropriate to the needs of the client; and

c.   Computer-stored data is limited, appropriate, and restricted to appropriate access.

10. Disagreements may occur and must be openly discussed with the goal of finding a win-win solution. Some degree of conflict (usually over content or process) will lead to improved understanding and performance as it will permit differences to be aired and satisfactory solutions found (Wilemon & Thamhain 1983). However, it is important to understand that <u>personal</u> conflict may not always be resolved, and steps may be needed to separate the conflicting parties.

11. Organizational staff and agents shall avoid placing themselves in a conflict of interest situation by requesting to be excused from the duties that may compromise their roles. In the case of a publicly funded organization, its operations must not only be fair, but also be seen to be fair. Every employee and agent of the organization must contribute to this ideal.

12. On occasion, some unethical practices may arise within an organization. The following are examples of unethical activities by employees who:

   a. have personal interests that conflict with organizational goals;

   b. use information available through the organization for personal gain;

   c. use their authority to influence decisions for clients;

   d. use their position to obtain benefits, services or programs offered by the organization to gain employment for their families or friends;

   e. become "obliged" to any person or organization that might profit from special consideration by the organization or counselor;

   f. offer preferential treatment to family members or organizations in which they have an interest;

   g. take advantage or benefit from information not available to the public during the course of duties;

   h. have a direct or indirect interest in financial leases to the organization (or counselor); and

   i. use position to obtain <u>financial</u> benefits for themselves, their families or organizations in which they have an interest.

Examples—Show me!

1. A client asks to see the training policy of an organization and is refused. He approaches the federal government with a ministerial inquiry and the organization is told to share this information with the client.

2. An organization keeps its hiring criteria a secret until a client complains and the organization is ordered by the federal government to publish this information.

3. The employment counselor's sister is granted funding even though she lives outside the office service area. A review of this decision after a complaint was made showed a conflict of interest existed and the client was deemed not eligible for funding. The result was that all funds paid were an overpayment; these funds were to be paid back to the funding organization. The employment counselor was disciplined.

4. An employment organization decided to run a survey on how many people in a local area were unable to work due to alcohol or drug addictions, to get an idea of the percentage of clients with issues in job maintenance. A college professor called the employment organization running the survey and asked to speak to the researcher involved to ascertain how the questions were weighted and who would be analyzing the results. When he learned that no one trained in research was in charge of the survey he advised them to stop the survey immediately and to destroy all responses.

Summary and Key Points—What is most important about this issue?

Employment counselors are bound by a code of ethics just as any persons engaged in serving the public. This code is designed to establish and maintain the integrity of such individuals in order to promote trust and confidence in service delivery. Such public servants are expected to understand clients' rights to privacy under the federal legislation as well as to promote access to information when such access is in order.

Self-Test Questions—How well do I understand this?

1. Why is it important that employment counselors are balanced in terms of the Medicine Wheel?

2. Why is it important to be a certified test administrator before administering tests to clients?

3. Why is it important for a counselor to be familiar with the Federal Privacy Legislation and Access to Information Acts as opposed to any provincial legislation governing privacy?

4. What is one ethical way of resolving a personal conflict between two staff members?

17

Labor Market Information

Chapter Goal—To be aware of and achieve balance in the supply and the demand for skilled workers in the local labor market and to share this information with clients.

Background—Important issues about this topic follow.
Important issues for employment counselors are to understand local supply and demand. Such issues normally relate to the type of clients that make up the local labor market in terms of gender, age, education, skills and the employment experience possessed compared to what employers demand when hiring employees. Employment counselors should identify the gap between what clients possess and what employers want and plan the best and most efficient way of filling that gap.

Some types of labor market information are:

- Occupational profiles (job duties, education, training)

- Wage rates

- Industry profiles (types of occupations being hired, location, prospects)

- Community profiles (what businesses, industries exist, including relevant data)

Motivation—Why do you need to understand this?

When the gaps in the local labor market are accurately identified, it is possible to focus education and training programs to fill those gaps more efficiently. The federal government provides funding to address the employment needs of Aboriginal people who are an under-employed target group, as well as to help satisfy employers' demand for skilled workers. The goal is to create a win-win solution and achieve balance in the local labor market.

Presentation—How does it work?

Current labor market information is needed to perform an environmental scan for the purpose of identifying industries with a high demand for skilled workers and those groups of unemployed requiring assistance to attain meaningful employment.

The federal government has targeted certain groups, on a national basis, for employment-related assistance. Such priority groups include persons with disabilities, youth, women, Aboriginal people and visible minorities.

Funding organizations prioritize additional local target groups, based on need, such as older workers and lone parents. Programs and services are then customized to accommodate the needs of these groups—both national and local—to ensure their inclusion in both the supply (providing skills training) and demand (linking them with jobs) side of the labor market. This could include partnership arrangements with other service providers to jointly deliver services that the funding organization, on its own, could not provide.

Other partnerships may be arranged with project sponsors (training providers) who supply skills development for high-demand industries. These industries could be contacted to discover the types of skills and competencies required for employment within their organizations. The funding agency could then create a strategy to develop economical training programs to meet the needs of industry demands with a trained supply of clients.

Clients should be provided with information sessions to create awareness of the current and forecasted local labor market conditions. This activity is part of the career decision-making dimension. Clients are then able to make an informed decision on an occupation in demand that is best suited to their personal and professional aspirations.

To keep the balance between both the supply and demand side of the labor market requires an awareness of the characteristics of the demand to compare them to those of the supply side.

The following diagram illustrates the need for community partners to join forces and share resources to assist clients in gaining the skills required for new employment opportunities that may be available within industry:

The Balance Between Supply and Demand

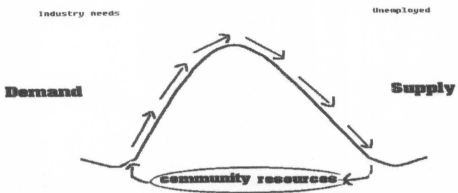

Arrows show clients' path from working to losing job & seeking help.

Industry, having a demand for skilled workers, hires workers and industry that is in decline lays workers off on the supply side. Most workers on the supply side who become our clients do not have the skills to re-enter the demand side on their own. They go through "community resources" to access the help they need to find work. Often this includes training, work experience, and other job finding assistance. Partners work together as "community resources" to help their clients.

A more in depth analysis of supply and demand having regard to the Medicine Wheel follows:

HEAD—Client characteristics include education and their capacity to be educated (intelligence). From an employer's perspective, education is one of the major qualifying/screening conditions for hiring someone into employment. Education is usually a prerequisite to appropriate skills training as in the case of apprenticeships. Generally, education is an important factor in labor market demand and supply.

HEART—Clients are happier and successful in jobs they like and in which they have an interest. Life is easier if one enjoys going to work. That is why it is important to match clients with occupations that will satisfy them so they will do well. Employers also want workers who like their jobs because they are motivated to work hard at their duties. Finding an occupation clients like to do is vitally important, making employment needs in the heart quadrant critical.

HANDS—Clients often have natural abilities and talents that may help them choose careers they will enjoy. They may find they are drawn to certain occupations and want to learn the skills required more than for occupations in which they have no interest. (Even though dad was an auto mechanic, the son may be more interested in being an airline pilot.) It will be evident that clients will not learn skills required if they are not interested in that occupation. Some may not do well as doctors or nurses because they cannot keep their "hearts from breaking" when the news is poor for their patients.

HOME—Some people will not be able to be fierce politicians or businessmen because they are not "hard nosed" enough to carry through a tough campaign or business plan. Values and beliefs may impact on occupational choices as previously discussed. For example, a Jehovah Witness may need to rethink a decision to work in the healthcare field in light of the requirement to administer blood transfusions. Political careers sometimes require that individual values and beliefs be put aside for the greater good.

Examples—Show me!

1. An employment office has trained some youth to become truck drivers without consulting with trucking employers. After six trainees successfully passed their training but were not hired, the employment office learned that the trainees were considered too young, for insurance purposes, to drive big rigs. Employers wanted to hire males, aged between 25 and 50 years old, who had no criminal records and a clean driving abstract. Insurance for adult males over 25 is significantly less than that for males under that age. The six teens who were trained were under 20 years old. If the employment office had consulted with the driving companies they would have learned the characteristics of the kind of workers the company wanted to hire.

2. An employer approached an employment counselor to ascertain if the organization would be interested in a project to train heavy equipment operators. The employment counselor was not sure so he consulted with the economic development officer and the provincial government, who both advised that there was a demand for heavy equipment operators due to demand in oil and gas and the forestry industries for the next 10 years. On this basis, a project where clients could be trained in heavy equipment operating skills and given the opportunity for employment was developed.

3. Before asking a client to make a career decision, it is the policy of the employment organization to ensure that local labor market information is provided. During the session, the skills that employers are demanding are described, as well as the education and institutional training requirements. Occupational profiles are shared with the client so he/she understands what the working conditions will be, the wages, as well as other important information about these occupations. The client then has an array of job types to consider before making an informed decision about one which might be suitable.

Summary and Key Points—What is most important about this issue?

Up-to-date local labor market information is a critical employment issue affecting clients' employment decisions. Any career decisions made without considering the local demand may fail to take advantage of the employment opportunities that could lead to a well paying, satisfying career. It is a key responsibility of an employment counselor to be aware of and to share local labor market information, in a timely way, with clients to enable them to make good decisions about employment issues.

Self-Test Questions—How well do I understand this?

1. If a client comes in to see a counselor and says he does not want to listen to labor market information because he has already made up his mind about the job he wants to do, what should the employment counselor do?

2. A review of local client characteristics shows that about 70% do not have the grade nine education usually required to enter any kind of occupational training. Why would it be important to learn about

upgrading institutions in the local area? Why would it be important to know specifically what grade level would be acceptable to enter into apprenticeship training? Why would it be important to find out what subjects would be mandatory for upgrading?

3. Why would it be important to explore a client's interests, talents and abilities during an interview for career decision making under the heart quadrant of the Medicine Wheel?

APPENDIX A

Definitions

Aboriginal Human Resource Development Agreement(AHRDA)—An agreement between an Aboriginal Employment and Training Authority and Service Canada (previously Human Resources Development Canada) to develop human resources through a mutually-agreed upon system of programs and services leading participants to desired results.

Accredited Institute—A recognized school or program providing training and services in accordance with standards set out by federal and provincial licensing boards.

Accountability—Being responsible for the efficiency, effectiveness and economy (the 3 e's of auditing) of all activities leading to desired results including client satisfaction.

Action Plan—A plan to complete appropriate interventions utilizing local Employment Assistance Service Agency services as well as those available in the community and through other government agencies that will lead to employment or self-employment, made through mutual agreement between the client and the AHRDA holder.

Active EI Claimant—An individual for whom an employment insurance benefit period is currently established with an active claim under the Employment Insurance Act.

Appeal—A timely written request by an appellant for reconsideration by an independent appeals committee of a decision by the AHRDA holder to deny a request for funding, outlining reasons for disagreement.

Appellant—A person who lodges an appeal against a decision by the AHRDA holder to deny funding.

Barriers to Employment—Obstacles experienced by clients preventing them from obtaining or maintaining suitable employment.

Capacity Building—The AHRDA specifies that this is the conscious use of financial, human and technological resources to enhance efficiency and effectiveness of labor market programming based on the ability to deliver and report on programs and services that meet the needs of the AHRDA holder, clients, employers and communities. For more details refer to the AHRDA document available on the federal government website.

Career Counselor—A licensed professional counselor who provides assistance (including therapy) to clients using a holistic approach to help them to overcome or deal with barriers in order to arrive at career decisions/interventions that satisfy the client's needs. (This could include mental "wellness" having to do with job satisfaction.)

Case Management—This is an approach that coordinates and supports activities for selected clients focusing on their needs and achievement of results. Such service is provided by a case manager to the AHRDA holder's clients as they progress through the steps of an action plan to completion.

Clients—Individuals eligible for the AHRDA holder's assistance with the understanding that the AHRDA holder is responsible for determining targets, developing eligibility requirements and selecting clients for orderly delivery of appropriate services and programs.

Client Characteristics—Individual or group descriptions of clients including: male, female, age, education, skills/occupational experience, disabilities, etc.. (Connector data base & the EI system can produce reports capturing client characteristics to help determine priority target groups for local labor market adjustment services and programs.)

Client Flow—The path clients follow from their first contact with the AHRDA holder and program deliverers to completion of all interventions including follow-up and measurement of results.

Communication Plan—A plan that covers information sharing about other plans, services, programs, projects, results, success stories and testimonials.

Conflict of Interest—A conflict between the private and the public obligations of a person in an official position.

Connector—A computer case management software designed by Alberta AHRDA holders to track and record client activities and results.

Consolidated Revenue Funds (CRF)—refers to training monies that are drawn from general tax revenue and therefore not specifically allocated towards proponents, contract agents or EI individuals.

Contract Agent/Agency—refers to a person or organization signing a formal agreement to provide employment services, training and/or programs to AHRDA holders in a specified way.

Cost Sharing—The sharing the costs of program and project initiatives among partners either through financial contributions or by donating "in kind" contributions of value to the program or project such as accommodation, equipment, services, etc..

Cost Effective—The measure of efficiency (appropriate duration for courses), effectiveness (appropriate material/curricula), economy (appropriate cost given duration and material/curricula) and satisfying client's needs.

Counseling Assessment—The process of determining if a client's personal barrier(s) to employment require the assistance of a counselor working in an appropriate specialty. A counselor may assist the client to overcome personal barriers before an action plan for becoming employed can be prepared. Once these personal barriers are overcome, the employment needs in the four employability dimensions can be assessed and addressed through an action plan that is then supervised by a case manager.

Counseling to Quit—Advice given to a client by a counselor to quit a job that does not pay enough to meet the client's needs, does not provide enough working hours to meet the client's needs, that has little or no chance of advancement, or that is otherwise unsuitable for the client, in order to allow a client to take training leading to work that will provide more security.

Decision Grid—A tool listing mandatory qualifications or eligibility requirements and desirable rating criteria used to evaluate pre-set criteria for the purposes of rendering a decision.

Dependants—Persons who are in the primary care of the client or participant.

Discretionary Authority—Personal judgment of staff designated to make decisions based on the factual information available and or where active EI clients are being referred to interventions in accordance with the EI Act to ensure adherence to Service Canada's policies.

Documentation—Written information provided by clients and/or other interested parties for the purpose of establishing eligibility and entitlement to AHRDA holder's programs, services and funding.

Double-Dipping/Double Funded—The act of an individual either knowingly or unknowingly obtaining funds from various sources for the same expenditures. If it is proven that the client knew, or should have known, that double funding was occurring, fraud charges could be laid.

Education Programs—Upgrading courses to allow clients to meet pre-requisites for entering occupational training and post secondary courses offered by colleges and universities to provide clients with professional certification.

EI Client—An unemployed person who, when requesting assistance under the AHRDA, is

1. an active EI claimant

2. a former EI claimant whose benefit period under the EI Act has ended within the previous 36 months, or

3. a former EI claimant for whom a benefit period has been established in the previous 60 months and who

    a. was paid special benefits under the EI Act during the benefit period

b. subsequently withdrew from active participation in the Labor force to care for one or more of their new-born children or one or more children placed with them for the purpose of adoption, and

c. is seeking to re-enter the Labor force.

Eligibility Requirements—Conditions that must be met by an AHRDA holder's clients to qualify for specific employment services or programs.

Employment Assisted Services—The Employment Assistance Service Agency staff provides employment counseling services to clients in the four employability dimensions.

Employment/Self-Employment Credit For Results Measurement—EI considers a client to have "found work" after twelve continuous weeks during which the EI client collected less than 25% of the EI benefit entitlement due to working. After this condition has been fulfilled, that client will be counted in the "employed/self-employed results" (even if the client later loses that job).

Employability Dimensions—These are broad competencies, skills and knowledge related to improving employability and through them to prepare for, to obtain and maintain employment. There are four dimensions used to categorize clients' needs to prepare for, obtain and maintain employment. These are Job Maintenance, Career Decision Making, Skills Enhancement and Job Search.

Employment Barriers—A counseling term referring to obstacles preventing a client from being able to prepare for, obtain or maintain employment. Examples: addictions, lack of life skills or education, unable to make a career decision, etc..

Employment Counselor—A person trained to assist clients who need to make decisions about employment under the four employability dimensions. When such help requires assistance to overcome barriers to employment, referrals may be made by the employment counselor to other certified counselors, including career counselors, addictions counselors and family counselors.

Employment Threatened—Where a person's work/employment is at risk due to either local labor market conditions that will cause closure of the job in the future and changing job requirements rendering a client unsuitable because she or he lacks skills, has outdated skills, or does not have certification that is now required for the job.

Entitlement—The right of an individual to access AHRDA holder's programs and services including funding support by virtue of being an Aboriginal person meeting established eligibility criteria.

Evaluation—The process of analyzing evidence to assess the quality/value of services, programs and performance against costs and results achieved. When efficiency, effectiveness, economy or client satisfaction is compromised, the service, program or performance may not be valuable.

Financial Assessment—For the purpose of income support, the process of reviewing a client's income compared to the projected costs of an intervention and determining the level of support that might be required.

Fiscal Year—For most organizations this is from 31 March to 1 April as opposed to the "calendar year" which is from 31 December to 1 January.

First Nations Person—A person who self-identifies as being First Nations.

Follow-up—Contacting clients at regular intervals (for example, 30—60 and prior to 90 days elapsing after they complete activities in their action plan, especially Skill Enhancement interventions, to document and assess employment results. The contact durations may vary and it is wise to consult Service Canada consultants to establish the current practice.

Results include feedback on whether the client is now self-sufficient in all four employability dimensions, if he/she found work or self-employment, or if she/he is in further training, if she/he abandoned their action plan and why, if action plan is incomplete or if unable to contact.

Found Work—Service Canada defines this as 12 consecutive weeks when the client collects less than 25% of their benefit rate due to employment. The AHRDA holder is not responsible for counting these weeks.

Full-Time Hours (Employment)—The amount of time normally worked in a full work-week by workers in a certain industry. This normally ranges from 35 to

40 hours per week. Some employers offer flex-time where workers work longer hours to earn time off.

Full-Time Hours (Training)—Normally 20 hours of training or more in a week is full time. Attending 3+ post secondary courses is also considered full time. (There may be no need for any income support if training is less than 16 hours per week.) Please note, Human Resources Skills Development Canada and Alberta Human Resources & Employment define full time training as follows: For academic upgrading, the client must have a minimum of 15 credits per term. For basic foundations, there must be a minimum of 20 hours per week. For short term skill training, the client must undertake 60% of the full course load. This definition agrees with the old federal and provincial policy as outlined in AECD Learner Assistance Operational Circular #7. NOTE: Discretion is in order when dealing with persons with disabilities who may require less hours over a longer period to succeed. See Persons With Disabilities Program Guidelines for details. Oteenow adheres to the training institution's determination of full-time status.

Good Academic Standing—Maintaining satisfactory progress as determined by the training institute.

Human Resource Skills Development Canada—A federal government agency that was responsible for delivering Employment Insurance income support to qualified, unemployed workers in Canada. It administered other programs such as Youth, Labor Market Services and support to Federal Provincial relations in certain areas. Recently this department has been renamed 'Service Canada' and has devolved many areas of its responsibility to provincial jurisdictions. Each province may have its own structure of responsibilities.

Income Support—Funding outside of actual course costs that is available to participants providing them with financial assistance in order for them to participate in employment training. Financial need must be demonstrated.

Incomplete Action Plan—closing a case before the action plan is complete for various reasons including:
    -the client changed his/her mind;
    -the client is no longer active in the labor market;
    -the intervention is no longer available; and
    -the client has been disqualified from further support.

Meaningful Employment—Long term employment allowing the client to participate fully in the labor market and achieve his/her full potential, achieving self-sufficiency.

Outcomes—A record of how each intervention (step) in an action plan ended regardless of whether a need under an employability dimension was or was not satisfied. (It may take more than one intervention to satisfy a need under one employability dimension.) Outcomes are measured by their effectiveness, efficiency, economy and client satisfaction and lead to desired results.

Overpayment—The amount of money/funds received by a participant to which he/she was not entitled.

Part I EI—The kind of benefits paid to clients who are on EI claims. The AHRDA holder has the authority under Section 25 of the EI Act, Part I to refer clients to suitable interventions while in receipt of EI benefits to the end of their benefit period. There can be no extension of these benefit periods. Only the actual benefit payments to the client payable through EI are charged to the Part I budget. EI service centers must be notified in accordance with the Aboriginal Human Resources Development Agreement (usually faxing required information) in order for an individual to stay on claim while attending training.

Part II EI—EI funds that are available for programs and services to clients who may now be receiving EI benefits or to clients who had established a claim within the last three years, or in the case or maternity/parental claims within the last five years known as "**Reachback**" clients.

Part II expenditures can include:

1. "top-up" Part I insurance benefits for active claimants

2. financial assistance for **Reachback** clients

3. financial assistance for active claimants whose benefits periods exhaust during the training

4. overhead costs associated with the delivery of employment services or training programs

All Part II expenditures are limited by the amounts allocated to the AHRDA holder.

Participants—The AHRDA holder's clients who participate in programs and services to increase their chances of finding employment or self-employment.

Partnerships—Generally, this refers to relationships that the AHRDA holder establishes with other entities concerned with the AHRDA holder's clients and the labor markets served by the AHRDA holder. These relationships may be formal, with signed agreements as is the case where funding occurs and accountability is an issue, or informal, where community or other players lend a hand or share "in kind" resources. In all cases, however, responsibilities of the partners are clearly outlined to avoid misunderstandings.

Part-Time Hours (Employment)—Hours that are less than full time. (Labor Standards defines part time working hours as less than 15 hours per week.) Where clients are employed part time, consideration must be made to determine if the client is underemployed.

Part-Time Hours (Training)—Where clients take training that:

-will earn less than 15 credits per term,
-is less than 20 hours per week (for basic foundations course)
-Oteenow adheres to the training institution's determination of part time status.
-is less than 60% of the full course load (for short term skills training)

Persons With Disabilities—Persons who self-identify that they have personal conditions that serve as barriers to normal participation in the local labor market.

Post Secondary—Studies offered by post secondary institutions for which the pre-requisite is a high school diploma or its equivalent.

Priority—Such demand and supply issues that are deemed by the AHRDA holder to have a major impact on the functioning of their local labor market.

Process—Steps to accomplish goals for certain functions including:

-Receiving and directing clients to appropriate services and programs,

-Service Needs Determination to identify client needs

-Case Management to help the client create and carry out an action plan that includes appropriate service and program activities leading to employment or self-employment

-Follow-up to assess and document results

Within these main processes there are a number of sub processes with their own steps such as using Connector, monitoring, appeals, etc..

Program Expenses—Costs related to training tuition, textbooks, supplies and income support.

Programs—The array of employment programs available to AHRDA clients offered by the AHRDA itself, federal or provincial governments and local community or private agencies/individuals, providing training and/or work experience through institutions, job sites and projects.

Proponents (Projects)—This term describes employers or incorporated organizations delivering work experience/training initiatives for AHRDA clients that will address the employment needs of clients leading to employment and relieving skill shortages in the community.

Quality Assurance—After decisions to grant benefits/assistance to clients/proponents has been made, the decisions and processes are reviewed to assess quality (including appropriateness of the decision, efficiency, effectiveness, economy and client satisfaction).

Quality Control—Before decisions to grant benefits to clients have been finalized, the quality of the decisions is reviewed so that control may be exercised by the reviewer to correct problems.

Reachback—A person who collected EI benefits within the last 36 months, and a person who collected special benefits (maternity or parental/adoption) in the last 60 months and is now seeking to re-enter the labor force. Service Canada can supply advice to establish if a client is a "**Reachback**".

Reception—The function of providing frontline service to direct, redirect clients to appropriate service and programs, answer basic enquiries, and address in-depth/case specific enquiries for response appropriately, assisting clients in completing applications, starting documentation, organizing, maintaining and assisting clients with labor market information needs.

Regional Bilateral Agreement (RBA)—A multi-year agreement (1996—1999) between Aboriginal Employment and Training organizations and the federal government to provide for the transfer of funds and authority to increase their prospects for employment or self-employment of Aboriginal workers by enhancing their skills. This was replaced by the Aboriginal Human Resource Development Strategy (AHRDS) starting April, 1999.

Resident—An Aboriginal person residing in the AHRDA holder's geographical area who may establish eligibility for funding.

Results—For the purpose of the AHRDA, results are defined in the AHRDA agreement setting out the numbers of EI and Non-EI clients who must become employed, self-employed and successfully complete employment-related training/experience interventions as well as dollar savings accrued to the EI and Income Support Program funds as a result.

Screening—automated or manual process for identifying targeted clients using established criteria such as youth, persons with disabilities and various skill shortage occupations.

Selection of Clients—The AHRDA holder "chooses" clients to assist in the four employability dimensions based on targeted priorities and the needs of the targeted groups, so that they may become employed or self-employed more quickly. Clients who are targeted in the the strategic plan are usually "selected" but non-targeted clients may also be selected for service and programs. Clients who are not selected are referred to self-service and in some cases, other agencies.

Self-Employment—Where a person works and earns remuneration by providing products and services to others in his or her own business organization. The degree to which a person is self-employed varies and depends on the hours spent in such endeavors, not necessarily on the amount earned.

Self-Sufficient—Clients who report their perception of independence and competence in conducting activities in the four employability dimensions without the assistance of an employment counselor or without using any of the AHRDA holder's sponsored programs and services, <u>and</u> the employment counselor validates the client's perceptions of self-sufficiency by reviewing the client's activities. Clients have achieved all goals set under the four employability dimensions and are capable of seeking employment independently without the support of a counselor.

Service Needs Determination—The process of identifying clients' needs in the four employability dimensions and assisting them to create an action plan with appropriate services and programs that will help them become employed or self-employed and attain self-sufficiency.

Special Needs—Clients whose needs require special additional attention, beyond those contemplated under the four employability dimensions. These needs may be physical or psychological and would be addressed through special arrangements designed to accommodate those needs. (Example: mentally challenged persons working by special arrangement at Safeway, restocking shelves in a supervised environment.)

Skills Development Program—Training programs that provide labor market skills to participants.

Skill Shortages—Skills that are "in demand" in the local labor or other labor markets that clients want to access.

Stakeholders—Any clubs, agencies, organizations or persons who have an interest in the outcomes of the AHRDA holder's products, programs, services, processes or clients. In the case of Oteenow, the stakeholders are Confederacy of Treaty 6 First Nations and Treaty 8 First Nations of Alberta.

Standards—Rules (based on benchmarks) set out by the AHRDA holder establishing how fast (speed of service) and/or how much (completeness/accuracy) or how many must be done within certain processes. This links directly to quality and client satisfaction. Examples: Connector guidelines that specify the mandatory blocks for filling and how soon client documentation should occur; follow-up with clients within specified time periods; speed of service processing applications; answering enquiries; paying benefits; processing appeals, etc..

Strategic Plans—The AHRDA holders decide how they will use their resources to develop clients having regard to the labor market(s) where they live and work. Such plans identify strengths, demands, weaknesses and surplus in the local labor market and establishes priorities, including targeting client groups to participate in strategies developed to assist the unemployed to find suitable work. Such plans focus on mutually-desired results for clients, the community stakeholders and partners, so that results satisfy all parties.

Suspension—A definite or indefinite period during which a participant is not allowed by the training institution or instructor to attend a regularly scheduled course of training activities.

Target Groups—Client groups chosen for attention by the AHRDA holders including:

-those whose characteristics make it very difficult for them to find work,
-high volumes of unemployed in a certain group who are impacting adversely on the labor market, and
-a shortage of occupational skills, locally.
The AHRDA holder has services and programs available that will assist clients. National target groups include youth, persons with disabilities and women. Local target groups may be chosen for attention in addition to these target groups.

Termination—A participant is dismissed from a course of instruction at an institution or by an instructor because of unsatisfactory progress and/or other compelling reasons.

Unemployed—Someone who is not gainfully employed or working at self-employment for fifteen or more hours per week and is seeking work.

Underemployed—Client is not working enough hours, or not getting enough remuneration, or not performing suitable duties or working under poor conditions not appropriate to the skill level possessed by the client.

Validation—A written record of the AHRDA holder's review of documents submitted by clients to establish their eligibility and entitlement to programs, services and funding available.

APPENDIX B

Canadian Ethnic Recipes

A. Creamy chowders (clam, corn)

B. Pea soup

C. Potato pancakes

D. Stew

E. Bannock

F. Meat Balls or Loaf

G. Turkey and Stuffing

H. Goose or Duck

I. Smoked Fish

J. Beef Jerky

A. Creamy Maritime Clam or Prairie Corn Chowder (Serve with bread & butter, if desired)

1. Parboil 3 cups diced potatoes and 1 cup diced carrots until firm in 3 cups salted water. Set aside both the vegetables and cooking water.

2. In a soup pot, sauté 4 strips bacon and 1 cup diced onion in ½ cup butter and 2 tbsp. corn oil. When the onion cooks to transparency and bacon is slightly crisp (<u>do not</u> drain off bacon fat) add ½ cup diced celery and ¾ cup flour; stir well to ensure all vegetables are coated and flour starts to brown. Do not allow flour to scorch.

3. To the ingredients in # 2, add 4 cups cold milk, 3—4 chicken or beef bouillon cubes, 1 tbsp. demerara sugar, 1/3 cup oyster sauce, and kosher salt to taste. Stir well to blend in the flour-coated vegetables and bacon. Add the potatoes and carrots in their cooking water and mix into the milk base. Add one small can of peas including the liquid. Taste to see if more salt is needed and add pepper.

4. For clam chowder add one small can of baby clams <u>and the clam liquid</u>. For corn chowder add a can of peaches and cream niblets corn including the liquid. Cook over medium-low heat until the chowder comes to a boil then simmer over low heat until it thickens, stirring constantly to prevent scorching. Remove from heat and add ¼ cup chopped parsley and let rest for 10 minutes before serving.

B. Pea Soup (French Canadian)

1. Soak 2 ½ cups split peas overnight in cold water. Rinse split peas in a sieve with cold water. Set side.

2. In a blender, put in 1 cup of water, 1 large onion cut into quarters, 2 garlic cloves, 2 medium carrots, 2 medium stalks of celery and blend until smooth.

3. In a large soup pot, put in the peas and the blended vegetables. Add a ham bone, 2 cups of diced smoked ham (or a scant tsp. of liquid smoke), 6 bouillon cubes (beef or chicken), 1/3 cup oyster sauce, and about 8 cups of cold water. Add some pepper but no salt. Simmer on low heat for about 3 hours, stirring every 20 minutes to prevent scorching. Adjust seasoning (salt, pepper) and serve with croutons, if desired.

C. Potato Pancakes—(Serve with sour cream & jam, or pea soup or sausage)

1. Peel and quarter 8 medium potatoes, (old starchy ones are best if available) and put them in a blender with one medium onion cut into quarters, 1 large clove garlic, 1 egg, ¼ cup canned milk or half and half cream, 1/3 cup flour (potato or rice flour if available, if not, use all purpose), 1 tbsp. fresh or dried chopped parsley. Blend well. The mixture may be a bit runny but it will hold together when fried. DO NOT ADD ANY SALT as it will cause the potatoes to turn black.

2. In a Teflon fry pan, on medium high, heat ¼ inch of oil until a drop of potato mixture sizzles and spoon out enough potato mix to make pancakes (about the size of a jar lid). The edges will be lacy. Lightly salt one side of the pancake, fry until golden brown and flip over, frying the other side until golden brown. Put pancakes on a plate lined with paper towels or a page of folded newspaper and allow excess oil to drip off for a few seconds before serving.

D. Stew (In this version no potatoes are used because their starch often makes the stew too thick and the flavor too bland. Serve them on the side)

1. In a large stew pot, add 3 tbsp. butter and 3 tbsp. corn or canola oil and sauté 3—4 cups round steak cut into bite sized cubes or use stewing beef

trimmed of excess fat, 2 cups carrots cut into thumb size pieces and 1 large diced onion.

After meat and vegetables are browned, add 1/3 cup flour and stir until all ingredients are coated and flour begins to brown.

2. Add cold water to cover meat and vegetables and stir until all flour is blended into the cold water.

3. Put in 4 beef bouillon cubes, 1 can of peas including the liquid, 2 cups of shredded cabbage, 1/3 cup diced celery and 1 clove garlic, if desired.

4. Simmer partially covered to allow steam to escape and to promote thickening of the gravy. If gravy is too thick cover up tightly for 20 minutes or so. Adjust seasoning by adding salt or pepper. (If a sweeter version is desired, add ¼ cup of ketchup to the gravy.)

E. Bannock Bread (by Charmaine Black-Gabriel)

1. In a large bowl, mix 6 cups flour, 2 tbsp. sugar, 6 tsp. baking powder and 1 tsp. salt.

2. In a second bowl mix 1 cup milk, 2 tbsp. oil, 1 egg and ¾ cup warm water.

3. Make a hole in the centre of the flour mixture. Add the wet ingredients. Stir slowly (about 4minutes) until the dough becomes soft and elastic, not sticky.

4. Grease and flour a baking pan. Flatten the dough to about 1 inch thick and place on pan. Perforate the dough with a fork. Bake at 350°C for about 25 minutes.

F. Meat Balls or Meat Loaf (Same meat mixture for both).

1. To two cups of medium or lean ground beef add 3 slices stale bread that has been moistened in warm water and wrung out, ¼ cup fine bread crumbs, 1 package dry onion soup, a few shakes of Worcestershire sauce, 1 tbsp. dried parsley and one egg. Mix well until all ingredients are blended well.

2. Shape into walnut-sized meatballs or into a loaf and put on a baking tray (meatballs) or into a loaf pan (meatloaf) and bake in the oven at

med. high heat 30 minutes for meatballs and 50—60 minutes for meat loaf.

3. Serve with gravy, or sauce or may be added to any soups you like to make a meal in a bowl.

   a. For Italian meatballs, add 1 tbsp. Italian seasoning and ¼ cup parmesan cheese to meat mixture. Serve with spaghetti sauce or in paprika gravy.

   b. For Swedish meatballs, add ¼ tsp. allspice and ¼ tsp nutmeg to meat mix. Put baked meatballs into a packaged beef gravy mix (prepared according to package directions) to which ½ cup sour cream, ¼ cup grape jelly (jam) and a dash if *Maggi seasoning has been added.

   c. For Chinese meatballs add 1 tsp thick, dark soya sauce, 1/3 tsp Chinese five spice powder, ½ tsp minced fresh green ginger, ½ tsp minced garlic to the meat mixture. Serve with sweet and sour or any other Chinese sauce.

   * Maggi is a liquid seasoning similar to Knorr liquid seasoning available at most grocery stores.

G. Turkey

1. Wash (and stuff the turkey if you like with your favorite stuffing), then lay it onto a sheet of wide, heavy duty tin foil (2 lengths or more, folded together). Brush the bird with melted butter and sprinkle one pack of dry onion soup over it if it is 12 pounds or less, or two packs for more than 12 pounds. Seal the turkey into the foil, put it into a roaster and bake at 350 degrees at 20 minutes per pound of turkey.

2. Open foil pouch for the last half hour of roasting time and brush with more melted butter. Turn up the heat to 450 degrees and allow the skin to brown. Ensure any stuffing is protected by foil covering.

3. Poke a hole in the bottom of the foil and carefully lift the turkey out of the roaster, keeping the turkey in the foil. Lay it on a cutting board to rest for 20 minutes. As you lift the turkey out, the juices will pour out into the roaster through the hole poked in the bottom of the foil. Make gravy by heating the drippings and adding a 'whitewash' (a mixture of

flour and water shaken up in a jar with a lid) to the drippings and simmer until desired thickening has occurred. Adjust seasoning by adding salt, pepper and Maggi.

H. Goose or Duck (An easy way to get a roast and some soup!)

1. After washing the bird, lay the duck or goose breast side down, into a roaster and add enough cold water to cover (if possible). Add 2 sticks celery, 2 bay leaves, 4 fresh sweet basil leaves (or 1 tbsp. dried sweet basil), 1 package dry onion soup mix, ½ tsp. sage, ½ tsp. poultry seasoning, 1 tbsp. parsley, 1 tsp. pepper, 1/3 cup oyster sauce, 1 tbsp. demerara sugar. Cover roaster and put into 375 degree oven. Allow it to simmer for two hours and then remove from oven. Let it cool for half an hour and then pour stock into a container to store in the fridge (remove/discard all the vegetables). Baste the bird by brushing it with fat from the soup stock, then add salt and pepper and return (in the roaster) to the oven. Allow the skin to brown and serve with orange marmalade, blackberry jam, raspberry syrup, cherry sauce, or other favorites.

2. After soup is cooled in the fridge, remove the congealed fat and add favorite vegetables and/or noodles and heat.

I. Smoked Fish

You need a smoker for this, or the recipe could be done on a barbecue using either the left or right burner turned on low over which one pan each of cherry, apple and hickory chips is placed, one pan at a time. (three pans of chips will be needed). Smoking time is eight hours and fish should rest for two hours after smoking.

1. Fillet the fish to produce two large fish fillets (with bones removed). Any type of fish may be used but salmon, white fish and northern pike are especially good.

2. Place fillets in a large gallon glass jar (the kind you get from bulk pickles) into which the following marinade is added: ¾ cup of salt (consisting of 1 part kosher or pickling salt to 3 parts table salt), ¾ cup white sugar, ½ cup brown sugar, ¼ bottle 'Johnnie's Seafood Seasoning', 8 cups water. Turn over every four hours for at least 24 hours.

3. One or two hours before smoking the fish, lay it out on a tray and dab it dry with a paper towel. Allow it air dry for an hour or so before arranging it on a rack (sprayed with cooking spray to prevent sticking). Put it into the barbecue on the side with the burner TURNED OFF opposite the side where the trays of wood chips will go. Otherwise, use the smoker following directions supplied for operating the smoker.

J. Beef Jerky
(Use the method similar to smoking fish but use sliced steak instead.)

1. Thinly slice (1/3 centimeter or ¼ inch thickness) partially frozen beef steak or cold, left over barbecued steak. Slice about 8 cups, and put slices into a container with a lid for marinating. Add: ½ cup thick, dark soya sauce, 3 tbsp. sugar, 2 tbsp. sesame oil, 1tsp. garlic powder, ¼ cup dried, bulk onion flakes, 1 tbsp. minced fresh green ginger, ½ tsp. pepper, ½ cup ketchup, ½ cup oyster sauce; allow to marinate overnight, covered, in the fridge.

2. One or two hours before smoking, lay the strips of meat out on a tray and dab them dry with a paper towel. Allow them to air dry for an hour or so before arranging on a rack (sprayed with cooking spray to prevent sticking). Put meat onto the barbecue on the side with the burner TURNED OFF opposite the side where the trays of wood chips will go. Otherwise, use the smoker following directions supplied for operating the smoker.

3. Check the meat after four hours, because depending on how thick and tender it is, it may be done sooner than four hours. This meat will need to rest too after smoking for a few hours. Store in re-sealable bags in the fridge or in the freezer.

APPENDIX C
Bibliography

A Problem Solving Process in Employment Counseling: Assessment and Follow-up. Human Resources Development Canada, June 1994

A Theory of Human Motivation and *Motivation and Personality*, 2nd edition, New York Harper and Row. Abraham Maslow (Also see businessballs.com a website offering free materials re the Hierarchy of Needs motivational model).

Communication dans la relation d'aide, Edition Etude HRW Itee., G. Egan, F. Forest

Counselling Guidelines for Measurement and Accountability in the CEC Employment and Immigration Canada (1993).Hull, Employment and Immigration Canada, Worker Programs and Services Directorate.

Counsellor Training in Canada: An Alberta Approach Journal of Employment Counselling: Special International Edition, vol. 30 (1993,) pp. 174-192.

Creating Smart Goals and *Attitude is Everything*. Paul J. Meyers

Employment Manual, Chapter 12, E.I.C. Employment and Immigration Canada (1993).

Getting To Yes, Second Edition. Roger Fisher and William Ury and Bruce Patton

Humanistic Psychotherapy: the rational-emotive therapy, McGraw Hill, New York. A. Ellis (1974).

Individual Employment Counseling an Action Based Approach from the Psychological Research Institute M.L. Bezanson, C.A. DeCoff, R.N. Stewart (1985).

In Search of Excellence. Tom Peters and Bob Waterman.

Sachez resoudre les problemes et prendre les decisions efficaces. S. Pokras (1989) Edition agence d'arc.

The Assessment Component of Employment Counselling. P. Patsula (1972) University of Ottawa.

The Assessment Process in Employment Counselling. C. Lecompte, L Tremblay (1987) Psychological Research Institute.

The Serenity Prayer. Reinhold Niebuhr.

Other Resources

The American National Employment Counseling Competencies: from the NATIONAL EMPLOYMENT COUNSELING ASSOCIATION, **a Division of the American Counseling Association (ACA) (See Website).**

Sample Code of Ethics for an Employment Counselor: (Generally based on a Proposal made by Wm. E Schultz).

Professor Norman Amundsen builds on The Grieving Cycle by Dr. Elizabeth Kubler-Ross; see web site: www.nobullyforme.ca/editorials.shtml

Legislation:

The Privacy Act
The Access to Information Legislation
Alberta Labor Standards
Canadian Labor Law
The EI Act and Regulations
Human Rights Act

978-0-595-44396-3
0-595-44396-6

Made in the USA
Middletown, DE
06 June 2022

66769979R00104